D1550829

QUAKERISM

A Spiritual Movement

❀

RUFUS MATTHEW JONES

1863–1948

Rufus M. Jones was known for many things—as teacher, author, philosopher, church statesman—but always as a Quaker. He was associated with Haverford College from 1893 to 1934. He edited *The American Friend* from its beginning in 1894 to 1912. He helped to organize the American Friends Service Committee in 1917, serving as Chairman or Honorary Chairman until 1948. He served as chairman of the All-Friends Conference held in London in 1920, aided in the organization of the Friends World Committee in 1937, and initiated the Wider Quaker Fellowship to maintain contact with "Friends of Friends." He was the author of more than fifty books and of contributions to the volumes of many others.

RUFUS M. JONES

QUAKERISM

A Spiritual Movement

Six Essays by
RUFUS M. JONES

❀

With a Sketch of His Life by
MARY HOXIE JONES

❀

Reprinted by
Philadelphia Yearly Meeting of Friends
1963

PRINTED IN THE U. S. A.

Foreword

RUFUS M. JONES (1863–1948) was known for many things
—as teacher, author, philosopher, church statesman—but
always as a Quaker. Outside the Society of Friends his vigorous, humorous, versatile personality, his thought and activity, contributed to the generally held image of Quakerism.
Within the Society he interpreted Friends to themselves, at
least in his own generation. Few earlier persons played this
role so extensively. One thinks of Robert Barclay and Joseph
John Gurney.

Although Rufus Jones wrote more than fifty books, few of
them explicitly present his conception of Quakerism. His
Faith and Practice of the Quakers (Methuen and Company, Ltd.
1927, reprint in paperback, 1958) was a popular summary.
The volumes he wrote for the historical Rowntree Series dealt
with particular persons and events and not primarily with the
nature of the movement as a whole.

The monumental Rowntree Series of the history of Quakerism and some of its antecedents had been planned with John
Wilhelm Rowntree as co-editor. After his untimely death it
was carried through by the survivor, with the notable contribution of two volumes by another English Quaker scholar,
William Charles Braithwaite. Rufus Jones as general editor
wrote introductions to each of the six works. They supply a
continuous and homogeneous presentation not so much of the
history of the movement as of its character.

It has seemed appropriate on the centenary of the author's
birth to bring these separate essays together in this reprint.

v

Their original text has been retained and occasional allusions or repetitions will be understood and allowed for by the reader. The convenience of having them all between the covers of one book will be appreciated by the older generation who knew them in the past or recognize in them the familiar style of their author; and newer generations may wish to know what was the understanding of Quakerism of one who exercised so great influence inside and outside its ranks.

The original publications of these introductions was as follows:

Studies in Mystical Religion, 1909
Spiritual Reformers in the 16th and 17th Centuries, 1914
The Beginnings of Quakerism, 1912
The Second Period of Quakerism, 1919
The Quakers in the American Colonies, 1911
The Later Periods of Quakerism, 2 vols., 1921

The first two volumes dealt not with Quakerism but with mystical and spiritual exponents of a similar religious approach. Their inclusion in the series served from the start to indicate some parallels and forerunners, if not the actual sources of Quakerism. The series was published by Macmillan and Company, London, between 1909 and 1921, with the financial assistance of the Joseph Rowntree Charitable Trust. When new editions of the third and fourth volumes by W. C. Braithwaite were published, in 1955 and 1961 respectively, by the Cambridge University Press, the introductions were omitted. Parts of the fifth volume were written by neighbors of the editor and fellow Quaker historians, Amelia Mott Gummere and Isaac Sharpless. It was reprinted in 1962 by Russell and Russell, in paperback.

Although a full biography of the author is available, *Friend of Life*, by Elizabeth Gray Vining (J. B. Lippincott Company, 1958) and an anthology, *Rufus Jones Speaks to Our Time*, edited by Harry Emerson Fosdick (The Macmillan Company, 1951, reprint in paperback, 1961), it seemed appropriate to prefix in this centenary volume the short and intimate biographical sketch prepared independently by Rufus Jones' daughter, Mary Hoxie Jones, and published in England (Friends Home Service Committee, 1955). The last named committee has courteously granted permission for its use as has the Joseph Rowntree Charitable Trust for reprinting the six introductions.

Perhaps some future occasion will provide opportunity for collecting some of Rufus Jones' other minor writings, published and unpublished, and for scholarly reappraisal of his thinking. Already in various quarters sundry hints of friendly dissent from some of his perspectives are heard. Meanwhile the unity and timeliness of the present reprint make it a fitting memorial of the 25th day of January, 1863, when, in the village of South China, Maine, Rufus Jones entered on his long and eventful life.

HENRY J. CADBURY

Haverford, Pennsylvania
November 1962

Contents

Foreword by *Henry J. Cadbury*   v

Rufus M. Jones, A Biographical Sketch,
by *Mary Hoxie Jones*   1

Introductions, by *Rufus M. Jones*, to
Studies in Mystical Religion   55

Spiritual Reformers in the 16th and 17th
Centuries   79

The Beginnings of Quakerism 119

The Second Period of Quakerism 139

The Quakers in the American Colonies 163

The Later Periods of Quakerism 183

Books by and about Rufus M. Jones 207

QUAKERISM

A Spiritual Movement

Rufus M. Jones

A BIOGRAPHICAL SKETCH

By Mary Hoxie Jones

Getting into the Right Furrow

Thomas Jones and Thankful his wife left Wales for the New World and settled at Hanover, Massachusetts in 1690. They were probably members of the Society of Friends, and their great-grandson Abel, who moved to Harlem, now called China, certainly was. Harlem was in the province of Massachusetts, but it was included in Maine when the state was established. He married in 1806 Susannah Jepson of Irish descent, and they began their married life in a log cabin at the north end of the lake known as the "Chiny Pond." The last seven of their eleven children were born in a new home, still standing, which Abel built in South China village. Edwin, his seventh son and youngest child, was Rufus Jones's father.

He married in 1852 Mary Gifford Hoxie who also belonged to a Friends family living in Albion, fifteen miles from South China, God-fearing stalwart people, who knew little of life's comforts and took its trials without complaint. Abel was a farmer who cleared seven farms, which means before he could plough a field or build a house he cut down the trees, removed the stumps, and made walls of the stones which the Glacial Age had left in abundance over the land. Mary Gifford

Hoxie's father, Matthew, was a cabinet maker in Albion, skilful with his hands, for he could fashion chests, beds or coffins according to the village needs. He was a man of humour, a kind of native wag, so his grandson and part-namesake came by his trait of humour naturally. Through the hard winters and the brief summers of this precarious, rugged existence, there was still room for laughter.

Edwin Jones brought Mary Hoxie to the family home to start her married life under the supervision of his mother, Susannah, and his sister, Peace. Here, in the front parlour, Rufus Matthew Jones was born on January 25th, 1863, a cold snowy night. He was the second son and third child, for Walter had been born in 1853, Alice in 1859. Herbert, four years younger than Rufus, was born in 1867. Edwin's second eldest brother, Rufus, had died late in 1862 so the baby was named for him and for Mary Hoxie's father, Matthew. Aunt Peace took the child in her arms and made her prophecy: "This child will one day bear the message of the Gospel to distant lands and to peoples across the sea."[1]

As a child he was always called Rufie and it was he who helped his father on the farm as soon as he was old enough. Walter had become a carpenter and gone away from home. Rufie was a good farm boy, learned quickly and soon became indispensable to his father. He took naturally to caring for animals and tilling the soil; at the same time he was happy at school or playing wild games with the village boys. Whatever was doing, Rufie was in great demand. There came the day, however, when he could neither work nor play. Like all the boys he went barefoot from the moment it was warm enough until the frost forced him to get into stiff, uncomfortable boots; and a bad bruise on his foot became an abscess. The local doctor, sharpening his lance on the nearest thing at hand, plunged it into the foot.

For nine months it looked as though Aunt Peace had been wrong about her boy's future. The infection spread from the foot to the leg and Rufus lay helpless on a couch in the living-room where the family took turns watching over him. But it was his mother who sat up with him at night holding his leg in her hands, trying to ease the pain and the fear of death which enveloped him. His grandmother and he read the Bible aloud together and she told him stories of her pioneer life. Aunt Peace knew that he could not die for he had a destiny. He was born for something great. And he recovered, learning to walk again, without even a limp. There is no doubt that this near approach to death and Aunt Peace's assurance that he would live to be a great person, gave him not so much a sense of his own importance as the feeling that he was being led forward by pillars of fire and cloud.

While he was ill, there was another prophecy. Their home was a way-station for Friends travelling in the ministry; in spite of South China's remoteness, an amazing number of persons visited there. James E. Rhoads, who later became the first president of Bryn Mawr College, rose one morning during family worship and laid his hand on little Rufus's head and said, "In this crooked and perverse world, this boy will be a shining light." The boy was deeply impressed, naturally, and "it filled me with a sense of awe as it tied in with Aunt Peace's prophecy. I never reminded James Rhoads in later years of this extraordinary utterance and had no idea, ever, whether James Rhoads remembered making it."[2]

Probably it was his mother who pondered over these sayings, for Rufus was an ordinary boy and showed little promise of ever getting into the trail she wanted him to find. Once, when he had seriously disobeyed her and he expected and deserved severe punishment, she took him to her room. Instead of telling him what she thought, she knelt in prayer, telling God of her hopes for this son of hers. It was a turning point in his life and although there were many failures, he was trying to be good.

He was needed on the farm and young Rufus knew he ought to stay and help his father. South China was home and he loved it. The beauty of the lake and the hills satisfied some of him, but not all. Something inside was driving him to a different life. As he and his father were hoeing potatoes one day, he stopped, leaned on his hoe and said that he must go away to school. The father's reply was the natural one, that Rufus had had all the education he needed for he had gone to every village school for miles around. Most serious of all, there was no money. The boy replied, " 'I know that well enough, but I guess if an American boy really wants an education, nothing's going to stop him.' 'If thee feels that way,' father replied, 'thee's free to go ahead. I've said all I can.' This decision marked another turning point and I dated my life from that moment."[3]

A scholarship was granted for him to attend the Friends Boarding School in Providence, Rhode Island, and at the age of sixteen-and-a-half Rufus Jones left home for this great adventure. He came home at Christmas because he was so homesick to see his mother, but when he came home again in a few months it was to attend her funeral. In 1882 Rufus Jones was able to enter Haverford College as a "second-year student."

EMBARKING ON THE SEA OF LIFE

When Rufus Jones graduated from Haverford College in 1885, he had to decide what he would do next. He was interested in studying law and yet he wanted to continue his studies in history and political science. Funds were available to him in either course. He had written his graduating thesis, at the suggestion of his much loved Philosophy teacher, Pliny Chase, on "Mysticism and its Exponents" and the research for this had strengthened his growing interest in history; it had, even more, indicated to him that there was a field which thrilled him beyond anything he had yet attempted.

At South China in the summer of 1885, he was faced with a choice between graduate work in history at the University of Pennsylvania in Philadelphia and a teaching position with a salary of $300 offered to him at Oakwood Seminary, a Friends Boarding School at Union Springs, New York (now called Oakwood School at Poughkeepsie, New York). He talked it over with Aunt Peace who was definitely inclined to choose the post at Oakwood for she understood teaching in a Friends School, whereas graduate work in a great university seemed terrifying to her. Rufus Jones weighed both opportunities. "I knew that, in real fact, I was choosing not so much a piece of work as *the kind of person I was going to be*, and that consciousness dominated the decision. . . . I felt pretty clear that I preferred the kind of self that would grow out of the year of teaching in a Quaker school—and I took the $300."[4]

For this salary Rufus Jones taught all the Greek and German, some of the Latin, astronomy, zoology and surveying. Besides his heavy duties in the school he found time to read Carlyle, George Eliot, Schiller and Goethe in German, English poetry and the mystics.

He had also begun his ministry in the Friends Meeting at Oakwood. "I felt now and then a clear, fresh message open up in my mind as we sat together in the silence."[5]

His first acquaintance with mysticism had been at family worship at home where "someone would bow and talk with God so simply and quietly that He never seemed far away. . . . The roots of my faith in unseen realities were reaching down far below my crude and childish surface thinking."[6] This was a daily experience; and besides this twice a week he went, from the time he was a baby, in the wagon or the sleigh to the meeting for worship in Dirigo, a few miles from the South China home.

Dirigo Meeting often had long, dreary silences, terminated sometimes by weird remarks repeated at every period of worship, or a stringing together of texts which gave no comfort to a small boy sitting on a hard form too high for his feet to reach the floor. Yet there were moments of thrill when Uncle Eli or Aunt Sybil rose, and with them the small boy's spirits. Rufus Jones was only ten when Aunt Sybil died, but he could never speak of her without a sense of awe and wonder, so marvellous was her gift, so rare her understanding, so close was she to God and the heavenly realms about which

she preached.   Uncle Eli was less dynamic; perhaps his feet
were more on the ground and his head not quite so near heaven.
He spoke of everyday things a boy could understand and he
made Bible stories come alive.   Uncle Eli and Aunt Sybil had
travelled over the world to visit Friends in England and other
far off places, and to bring the Gospel to those in darkness,
places that Rufus, some day, hoped to visit.

Aunt Peace and his own mother were his daily, intimate
companions and they knew God as their present Friend.   The
boy, Rufus, had lived among mystics and had not known them
by that name, but his senior year at Haverford and the work
on his final thesis made him aware of the fact that mystical
experience was not only something in history but something
he had always known in his own life.   The year of teaching
at Oakwood served to strengthen his intellectual and spiritual
life.   It also brought him Sallie, who was likewise a teacher
there.

"I have just come home from Meeting, where Uncle Eli
preached one of the most powerful sermons I ever heard.   The
thrills ran up and down my back.   He preached from my old
text, 'The word that came to Israel at Kadesh-barnea, *Go
Forward.*'   As he stood there with his grey locks and trembling hand, and got filled with fire as he went on, I felt that he
himself was a prophet, who was receiving messages from
above for the people.   I am getting some of Uncle Eli into
my life."[7]   Thus Rufus Jones wrote from South China at the
age of twenty-three, to Sarah Hawkeshurst Coutant, twenty-
four years old, who became his wife two years later.

Sallie Coutant came from a Huguenot family living in
Ardonia, near Poughkeepsie, New York.   She had been a
student at Oakwood Seminary and returned as a teacher the
year before Rufus Jones came.   They were both filled with a
passionate love for truth, for education, for making their
lives pure and good.   They both came from small, country,
Quaker homes where poverty was a reality, but where a
homespun culture and dignity were equally real.   They had
both lost their mothers and yearned for an understanding soul

with whom to share all the gropings which young people have.

When he wrote to Sallie on August 7th, 1886, he had an important piece of news. "My European blossom has become a seed which is fast ripening. I propose to go to Europe for a year, spending most of the time getting the French and German languages. I am arranging to go . . . two weeks from Thursday. Of course there will be many hard things to endure and a great many lonesome days to be spent, before the year is over, but I think I can stand it, for I have looked on all sides of the question and it looks right."

No sooner had he made this decision than another opportunity came to him. "I have had the position of principal of Damascus Academy, Ohio, offered to me, which would be a good place, but having put my hands on the plough handles and having the horses nearly harnessed, and furthermore feeling that I am in the right furrow, I do not think it best to turn back. I never felt so much in my life before that I had reached the dividing line between past and future, boyhood and manhood as I have this summer. Sometimes when I stop and listen I can almost hear the infinite sea of life roar and rumble and I know that everything is shouting in my ear, 'embark on it,' and I mean to obey the voice."[8]

Hannah J. Bailey of Winthrop, Maine, loaned Rufus Jones the money for this momentous journey and Uncle Eli provided him with letters of introduction. Before he sailed from New York on the steamer *Pennsylvania* on August 26th, he visited Sallie at Ardonia and they reached an understanding with each other, although no engagement was announced.

He landed at Glasgow and after a few days in Scotland among strangers he wrote from Wilmslow in Cheshire: "I am now at the 'Mecca' toward which I have been tending and if I were in my father's house I could not be made more at home. I am with Ellen Clare Pearson who went to Palestine with Uncle Eli and Aunt Sybil, and this is my home for a week. Uncle Eli's name is like 'Open Sesame' at every Friend's house. I had never expected such welcomes as I get, and my friends here have written to friends in the cities which I am to visit, so I shall not feel so much like a stranger as I did in Scotland."[9]

William Lean, then Headmaster of Ackworth, entertained Rufus Jones. Fielden Thorp met him at York station and Rufus Jones "felt at home with him at once. . . . [At York Meeting] I spoke briefly [as did Fielden Thorp]. It did me good to have him say what he did and after Meeting he said some very kind things to me. I went at once to York Minster, the greatest cathedral in England. It is impossible to describe such a structure and the impression it makes. Fielden Thorp gave me a splendid letter of introduction to John Bright, so I started for Rochdale and soon found the home of 'the great commoner.' The door opened and in came a cat followed by two dogs and the dogs by the real John Bright who looked just as his pictures do. A grand, good face, crowned with snow-white hair."[10]

He visited Birmingham, "where I was met by Richard Barrow who took me to his lovely home at Edgbaston. I attended a Bible school of three thousand members and a very large meeting on First Day. I was called on to address the school, was introduced as a nephew of Eli Jones."[11] It was at Bull Street Meeting that Rufus Jones "rose trembling, to speak,"[12] and said that since sitting in this meeting he had been thinking. What his message was, no one remembers, but a Friend took him aside at the close and told him, "*Thou shouldst not have been thinking.*" The young visitor took this in good grace and the remark became a family saying for the rest of his life but it might have wrecked his ministry, for such an eldering in such a place was a serious matter. Fortunately, Richard Barrow and the daughters of Joseph Sturge encouraged Rufus Jones.

From Birmingham he travelled to Stratford, Warwick and Oxford on his way to London. "Nothing pleased me more [in Oxford] than the monument at or near where Latimer, Ridley and Cranmer were burned. They have always been my heroes. Latimer's last words are grand: 'Be strong, Master Ridley and play the man, for to-day we will, by the grace of God, light such a candle as shall never go out!' "[13]

In London he made his headquarters with Hugh Fox. One of his great moments was a chance to hear Spurgeon. "He *believes* in God, and I think he lives and walks with him."[14]

He did a good deal of sightseeing with William Charles Braithwaite, also twenty-three years old, as his guide. "I have seen the most important and interesting things in London, I was with Bevan Braithwaite two nights, one with Stafford Allen."[15]

Before the London visit was over, Rufus Jones was joined by Charles Jacob, his intimate cousin, a boyhood companion, and school and college friend. They had planned this trip together. The two young men arrived in France early in October, going first to the little town of Dieu-le-fit, south of Valence, where they stayed together for a month. It was here that Rufus Jones had a mystical experience and felt "the walls between visible and the invisible suddenly grow thin, and I was conscious of a definite mission of life opening out before me. . . . I remember kneeling down alone in a beautiful forest glade and dedicating myself then and there in the quiet . . . in the presence of an invading Life, to the work of interpreting the deeper nature of the soul and its relation with God."[16]

Early in November he left Charles Jacob and moved to the home of Jules Paradon, a member of the small group of French Quakers in Nîmes, where he struggled alone with climate, food, poor health and homesickness. "I wish I could wake up and find myself sitting on the floor of my room at Haverford, but I must not look back for fear of becoming a pillar of salt."[17]

Charles joined him later, but they left Nîmes together in February 1887 for Geneva which he thought the most agreeable city he had yet seen, and, after a short stay, leaving Charles there, Rufus Jones went on to Heidelberg where, in a delightful boarding home, he found "the food splendid and everything neat and homelike. It is not cold and I have a stove in my room."[18]

Spring in Heidelberg was almost idyllic; for a time his health was better and many of his doubts vanished, but he was nagged by the uncertainty of his future. This year was to prepare him to be a better language teacher, but he had no teaching post. Sallie had told him there was a place open at Oakwood, but there was no definite letter offering the position. In any case, he did not really want to go back there; he wanted to teach at the Friends School in Providence, where his first cousin, Augustine Jones, was the principal.

"It is not easy to be good," he wrote. "How do great souls decide their all important questions so quickly? Their whole life has been preparing them for the moment. I have fought, more than one would think. I do not always succeed, but I am in earnest in this business and I do not intend to be a knot in the tail of the devil's kite to help it fly. . . . Sallie, thou knows that I aspire to be something and do something, what it shall be I do not know but this I know, that he who would ease the burdens of the world must himself breathe the 'ampler aether and diviner air.' The day is past when to be good means to wear grey clothes and a long face. If any man is to be loaded with sunshine it is he who feels himself at peace with the world and its Creator."[19]

In the next few days a letter from Augustine Jones arrived and on April 26th Rufus Jones wrote accepting the position.

With this important matter settled, Rufus Jones looked forward to the future, "the more I think of it the more I rejoice that I am going to Providence,"[20] and he was eager to get home. He felt more sure of himself than he ever had. He was now certain that he was not going to be always a teacher of history nor of languages. During his weeks in Heidelberg he had studied under the great philosopher, Kuno Fischer. "My interest in mysticism had been steadily growing and deepening, and now I saw that the best approach to an understanding of this great human experience was to be found in philosophy and psychology. . . . When I finished Fischer's courses and went on to Paris for my final work in French, I had my mind already made up to turn henceforth to the study of man's inner life and the spiritual ground and foundation of the universe.''[21]

He was twenty-four years old and life was promising much as he started the voyage back across the Atlantic. He was getting well into the right furrow.

TESTINGS OF FAITH

The two years at Providence were happy ones. His letters to Sallie before they were married indicate how deeply he loved his teaching, and that pupils came willingly and eagerly to his class-room. He took an important part in the school meeting for worship and he was becoming more and more interested in American Quakerism. In the autumn of 1887, when his Uncle Eli returned from the conference in Richmond, Indiana, where Bevan Braithwaite and several other British Friends had been in attendance, he saw Rufus Jones and told him about the conference and its meaning for the Society of Friends. It was at that gathering that the ''Richmond Declaration of Faith'' had its creation. There can be no doubt that Uncle Eli's reports fired Rufus Jones with enthusiasm to take part in the Quaker movement. Another important visit of this time was a day spent with John Greenleaf Whittier, then an old man living in Danvers, Massachusetts.

Rufus M. Jones and Sarah H. Coutant were married at her home in Ardonia, New York on July 3rd, 1888, and after a brief visit to South China, Maine, they came to live at the Friends School in Providence. He had taught there as arranged, during the year 1887–1888, but the marriage was postponed until he could earn enough money to return what had been borrowed for the trip abroad.

During this summer he started his first book, *Eli and Sybil Jones, Their Life and Work*, published in Philadelphia in 1889. This first attempt at anything longer than an article must have given him pleasure. It gave him a chance to study and interpret the lives of two persons who had meant much to him, and to begin his work on Quaker research and history.

At the end of the school year in 1889 Rufus and Sarah Jones

packed up their possessions and moved to the Oak Grove
Seminary, Vassalboro, Maine, where he was to be Principal.
Oak Grove was ten miles from South China and was, like the
school in Providence, a Quaker boarding school for boys and
girls, under the care of the Yearly Meeting of Friends for New
England.

He and Sallie stayed at Oak Grove for four years, he as
principal, teacher, minister, man of all work, counsellor,
companion.   The men and women who were his students still
speak of those years as wonderful for them.   Sallie was housekeeper, and part of the time his brother Herbert was the
business manager.   Even with all this help it was, for him, a
twenty-four hour a day job, with breakdowns in the windmill
always occurring just before Meeting.   He looked back on
those years and said, "I could only thank God . . . that He had
led me hither and had laid all these tasks and responsibilities
upon me.   Through them I had learned the deeper meaning
of life, and I had in a new way found the hidden sources of
power to live by."[22]

Here at Oak Grove, on January 23rd, 1892, their son,
Lowell Coutant Jones, was born, two days before Rufus
Jones's twenty-ninth birthday.   The baby was named for the
poet, James Russell Lowell.   This experience of holding the
new-born child in his arms remained forever a supreme moment of his life.   "I never got away from this divine miracle."[23]   Between Lowell and his father there always was a
special bond, and the father found in this boy not only the
new expression of himself, but a new revelation of God's love.

Once again a challenging opportunity came.   In 1893 Rufus
Jones was asked to come to Philadelphia as editor of *The
Friends Review* and he agreed if a way could be found for him
also to do some teaching at Haverford College.   The President, Isaac Sharpless, teacher and dean during Rufus Jones's
student days, welcomed Rufus Jones to the faculty, to give a
course of lectures in philosophy.   Living quarters were found
at the college for Rufus and Sallie and baby Lowell.

The Friends Review, founded in 1847, had started "in the

midst of a disastrous Quaker controversy . . . [and] represented in the period of its birth, the 'evangelical or progressive' section of the Society of Friends in America. It especially appealed to those who were in sympathy with the
famous English Quaker leader, Joseph John Gurney. . . .
The Friend of Philadelphia was the conservative paper, expressing in large degree the ideas and ideals of those who
were popularly called 'Wilburites,' so called because of their
sympathy with John Wilbur, the stern opponent of Gurney."[24]

Much of this controversy was a dead issue before Rufus
Jones became editor, but he inherited a complicated task for
there were many Friends who had little understanding of
what the various issues were. Rufus Jones had grown up in
South China under the influence of evangelical ministry although there was much in his Meeting which would seem to
have been conservative. It was fed by the living waters of
Gospel ministry and there was none of the dissension and bitterness which tore at the vitals of the Friends Meetings
farther south in New England. The Hicksite-Orthodox separation which took place in Philadelphia in 1827 had affected
other areas but had not touched Maine. In his childhood,
Rufus Jones had little idea of the troubles there were, but in
his student days, both in Providence and in Haverford, he
began to see what havoc had taken place. He never really
became aware of the state of American Quakerism until he
started writing editorials each week for *The Friends Review*
and letters came pouring back to the editorial office on Seventh
and Arch Streets, Philadelphia.

The Friends who made up the *Review's* Board of Managers
were older than he—statesmen, with whom Rufus Jones had
the happiest relationship. James Wood of Mt. Kisco, New
York, perhaps his dearest friend in this group of men, played
a leading part in the creation of the Five Years Meeting in
1902, and Rufus Jones worked closely with him during the
years of preparation for this event.

Philadelphia Yearly Meeting (Race Street) featured little
in Rufus Jones's life until much later. But some members

of Philadelphia Yearly Meeting (Arch Street) looked upon him as dangerous. He wore a moustache, a frock coat, he preached about thinking, anathema to Arch Street Friends in the 'nineties' as to some Friends in Bull Street in the 'eighties,' he represented modern thinking and higher criticism of the Bible.

Had Rufus Jones desired to bring his membership to Philadelphia from China Monthly Meeting and Vassalboro Quarterly Meeting, subordinate bodies of the Yearly Meeting of Friends for New England, where he had been recorded a Minister of the Society of Friends in 1890, he probably would not have been accepted. By the time such a transfer might have been acceptable he was deep in the life of the Five Years Meeting to which Philadelphia did not belong, and he had no desire to make any change in his membership.

It was Rufus Jones's purpose, in *The Friends Review* " to promote in every possible way 'the advance of Christian Truth' . . . and to maintain and honour *spiritual realities* rather than *forms and traditions*."[25]   Forty years later he could say, "I then foresaw the profound testings of faith that were to come with the new century and . . . I was prepared to meet them calmly and fearlessly."[26]

Fearless he always was. It was not so easy to keep calm. Week after week he wrote his editorials interpreting what he believed to be the essence of Quakerism—the great Quakerism which rose above petty differences or power complexes or ingrown lives. Some letters to the editor expressed shocked and horrified sentiments of the writers and some Friends discontinued their subscriptions. But there were many readers of the paper who were enthusiastic, hearing, at last, the ringing tones of a prophetic leader. There was no doubt that a new voice was heard in the land.

After a year's editorship, encouraged by his supporters, Rufus Jones in 1894 made the daring step of merging *The Friends Review* and *The Christian Worker* into a new paper— *The American Friend*. *The Christian Worker*, published in Chicago, was a western version of the *Review*. On his initiative and with diplomacy and patience and the help of older and wiser associates, the union was brought about. On July 19th the first issue of the new paper appeared and his first editorial said, "The religious journal that becomes a power for good must do more than reiterate constitutional beliefs and universally accepted views; it must be an educational power, a help to spiritual growth, marking a continual advance in thought. *It must not be narrowly bound to expound the traditions of a section, a party, or a creed.*"[27]

One Philadelphia Friend who found him particularly annoying referred to him as "that man Jones," a term of opprobrium representing the opinion of many Friends throughout the United States. "That man Jones" was shaking the complacent, disturbing the smug, shaming the lazy and they didn't like it. The beauty and the power of the living Christ filled the soul of this young editor just as these experiences had thrilled George Fox and his great succession of torchbearers.

Rufus Jones not only dreamed what might come to the Society of Friends. His life was not just writing and theorising. He went from his editorial desk to the classroom where he faced young men, only a few years younger than himself, and here he expounded philosophical truths of the ages. He also had their insistent questions. He lived all the time among young people. Life was good and its opportunities were endless.

He had amazing vitality and vigour in spite of hay fever, frequent colds and occasional periods of complete physical and spiritual exhaustion. Nearly six feet tall he had a tremendous stride as he walked from his home to the college class-room or to the railway station at Haverford for a train to his office in Philadelphia. These two jobs demanded great physical energy as well as mental and spiritual, and either one would have been full time for most people.

In addition he spoke more and more often in Meeting, on Sunday, and on Thursday as well when all the college students were required to attend. He was giving lectures in the neighbourhood and he began his travels to distant places. In order to know more intimately the types of Friends who subscribed to *The American Friend*, he took a trip to the middle west where he visited Meetings and stayed with Friends in their homes. He had to write his editorials on trains and whenever he could find a minute. Thus began his peripatetic life which took him into the heart of American Quakerism and into the hearts of its members.

A Heavenly Meeting

Rufus Jones came to England in 1897, just eleven years after his first visit. The second journey was made possible by David Scull, one of Rufus Jones's special friends among the group backing *The American Friend*. There were various obstacles in the way of the journey, for he did not want to leave Haverford College before the end of the academic year which would be necessary in order to reach England in time to attend London Yearly Meeting, and he did not want to be away from his wife, for he was anxious about her health. She found the Philadelphia climate difficult and had constant attacks of bronchitis, but there was no hesitation in her mind and she urged him to accept the invitation.

Sarah Jones was in every way a helpmeet and companion for her husband. She had helped him at Providence, she had been the housekeeper at Oak Grove, and when she came to Haverford and they had a home of their own after two years of rather make-shift arrangements, she added to the meagre salary by taking boarders. There was nothing slipshod about her and she was a meticulous housekeeper. She worked hard to have things just right and she also found time to help her husband with his editorial work. The only way he could leave for England was by handing to her the oversight of the paper. It was understood, however, that she and Lowell would spend the weeks of Rufus Jones's absence somewhere in a better climate in the hope that her cough would improve.

Rufus Jones departed for England with a heavy heart

While he was gone he felt constant anxiety for Sallie; her letters told all too little about her health. He kept wondering whether he had done right to come and was tempted to return home.

Arriving at Liverpool, after a brief visit with Irish Friends, Rufus Jones received from Rendel Harris, a warm welcome and the message "Are thee there, Rufus?"[28] After London Yearly Meeting Rendel Harris agreed to go with Rufus Jones to Switzerland and this dear friend proved to be an ideal companion. As Rufus Jones himself wrote, "he had a fascinating personality, a charm of manner, a striking style both of speech and pen."[29]

A walking trip was planned so that they would reach Mürren on Sunday, June 20th, when Rendel Harris knew members of the Rowntree family would be there, among whom was John Wilhelm Rowntree. During a spell of severe weather, Rufus Jones says in a letter to Sallie, "We are now all together and we have had some most valuable talks together. I am especially glad that during this dreadful weather we can sit and talk over the vital questions of Quakerism. We had a beautiful meeting this morning, there were fifteen of us Friends. John S. Rowntree (father of Arnold S. Rowntree), Rendel Harris and I spoke and prayers were offered. It was a heavenly meeting."[30]

Thirty years later he wrote that John Wilhelm and he "spent most of that Sunday finding our intellectual and spiritual contacts, reviewing our past lives and forecasting possible plans for the future." The next day they climbed the Schilthorn and "walked much of the way together side by side, talking eagerly of plans for the future. . . . It was a day of continual thrills—my first experience on a high snow mountain—but greater than the joy of climbing or of seeing sunrise on the Jungfrau . . . was my highborn joy as I went on discovering the remarkable character and quality of the new friend who was walking by my side. We both knew before the day was over that we were to be comrades for the rest of life."[31]

John Wilhelm Rowntree, five years younger than Rufus Jones, was even in 1897, at the age of twenty-nine, ill with the terrible kidney disease which was threatening his eyesight, his hearing and his life.

Both these young men were thrilled with the history of the Society of Friends and the potentialities which they saw in Quakerism as a movement. They had managed to throw off some of the strangling, smothering aspects which had tended to destroy the dynamic force of the Society, and they had each come into the experience, as did George Fox, of knowing God experimentally. Each felt that he had a special part to play in this great movement and what could they not do if they worked together? Rufus Jones loved to quote Wordsworth about the French Revolution, "Bliss was it in that dawn to be alive; to be young was very heaven."[32] So, too, was it at that moment to be a Quaker and to find John Wilhelm Rowntree.

Together they planned to write the history of mysticism and of Quakerism. One Summer School, to be held later in that summer of 1897, could lead to later ones. They saw the need for young Friends, seeking like themselves, to have opportunities for study, discussion and worship together, and they began to plan ahead.

A Closed or an Open Door?

On the voyage back to New York Rufus Jones's mind was filled with these new mountain-peak experiences. When he reached New York in July, however, his whole world broke around him. Sallie had struggled with her coughing spells and realised she was not getting better. She took Lowell to his grandparents in Ardonia and then she visited a doctor. The result of this visit she reported in a long letter which greeted her husband on his arrival in New York. Sallie's illness was no longer bronchitis but tuberculosis and the doctor was sending her to Saranac Lake in the Adirondack Mountains.

This was a staggering blow. Rufus Jones had always urged

her to take care of herself, and to work less strenuously in the care of the home so as to keep strong and well. Now he was determined that she should be cured. He could not leave his work but he managed to come to Saranac, an overnight journey, for occasional week-ends. During the summer of 1898 he spent his vacation with her, a distressing time, for she was obviously no better. They tried to buoy each other up with a hope which neither one really felt. Rufus Jones was distraught both about Sallie and about Lowell, lest he should become ill too, and he spent sleepless nights trying to believe that Sallie could recover, knowing, deep down, that her case was hopeless. But he kept up a brave front when he visited her and when he wrote her his daily letter. In the autumn of 1898 she moved to her father's home in Ardonia because she felt she would be too great a burden of care for her husband. This was a hard decision. Lowell remained with his mother for a short time, but she was too ill and it seemed best for him to come back to Haverford.

Sallie died on January 14th, 1899. Her death left Rufus Jones with a heavy heart. He, and Lowell even more, needed her love, help and care. Now the father had to be mother as well for the little son. Utterly devoted to each other, he and Lowell started life over again in their home at Haverford. Fortunately he had work which occupied all his time.

Teaching at Haverford College was becoming a more and more important part of his life. He was by this time doing most of the work in philosophy and psychology. His work as editor also increased and the many responsibilities for American Quakerism crowded in upon him. He was working constantly with James Wood on drafting a plan for uniting some of the American Yearly Meetings in what later was called the Five Years Meeting. In 1900 the draft Discipline to be used by this body appeared in *The American Friend* for comment and criticism, of which there was a great deal. The first sessions of the Five Years Meeting were planned for 1902.

The first American Summer School was held at Haverford

College in 1900, to which several British Friends came, including Rendel Harris and John Wilhelm Rowntree. Rufus Jones had done much of the preparation for the Summer School and had written five lectures, later published in book form, entitled *A Dynamic Faith*.

American colleges and universities allow the members of their faculties to take a sabbatical leave, every seven years. Rufus Jones spent the year of 1900–1901 at Harvard University, doing graduate work with the great men who were there, Hugo Münsterberg, Josiah Royce, George Herbert Palmer and George Santayana. "For the moulding of my intellectual outlook in this period I owe most to my teachers at Harvard. . . . A year's work in that 'Philosophy Four' course [with G. H. Palmer] came nearer to being a 'complete education' than any other course of study I have ever known."[33] During that year he took three courses in philosophy and one in the New Testament. Lowell spent the year happily at the Friends School in Providence and was near enough to Cambridge for father and son to have frequent week-ends together.

Rufus Jones came to England for the Scarborough Summer School in 1901, bringing Lowell. He gave a Sunday evening address at Scarborough. "I felt I made a mess of it but the oddest thing was, it had a marked effect on so many people. Some date their interest in Quakerism from that moment. Something outside of myself happened."[34]

Rufus Jones was deeply appreciated in England but he was still being criticised and misunderstood in America. It was hard work to awaken Friends in that great country. While he was at Scarborough, a post-card brought this message written by an Iowa Friend. "I write to ask thee to stop my paper. I trust that I and my family believe the Bible is divinely inspired from lid to lid, and therefore do not want a paper coming into my home that begins to smell of the Pit. *The American Friend* is doomed if it does not get right with God soon."

His sorrow and loneliness made these attacks harder to bear than they had been. In England he found a different atmosphere and almost he wished he might remain there. The opportunity to do so was coming in the very near future but on his return to Philadelphia his mind was well occupied with other, more urgent matters.

As early as 1900 Rufus Jones was corresponding with a young Philadelphia Friend, Elizabeth Bartram Cadbury. She had written, at his suggestion, a full account for *The American Friend* of a trip to Palestine which she and several other Philadelphia Friends took in the winter and spring of 1900. The number of letters was increasing and by the summer of 1901 Elizabeth Cadbury was writing fairly frequently to "My dear friend, Rufus M. Jones." She seemed to take much interest in the progress of the Scarborough Summer School. Not very long after his return, the "dear friend" is dropped and the letters begin "Dearest Rufus." On November 19th, 1901, David Scull, an intimate friend of Elizabeth's father, wrote to Rufus Jones, "I have heard with great pleasure of thy engagement. Happiness would seem assured with such a wife as thou art securing. With excellent mental qualifications are joined in her the priceless blessings of the influence of a godly home life and a good solid Quaker training. I am glad to believe that thy life will be yet fuller and richer with such a helpmate in thy burdens."

Lily, as she was then called by her family and close friends, was born on August 15th, 1871, and was the eldest child of Joel and Anna Kaighn Cadbury of Philadelphia. Her grandfather Joel, having come from England to visit his aunt, fell in love with her daughter—his first cousin—Caroline Warder. Friends at that time did not permit first cousins to marry, and this young couple were disowned, but fortunately the Monthly Meeting decided it had made a mistake and some years later Joel and Caroline Cadbury were taken back into membership. The tie between the families in England and America was strong; visits and letters back and forth kept the parents and children acquainted.

Rufus Jones and Elizabeth Cadbury were married on March 11th, 1902, in Philadelphia. Thus began the forty-six years of their wonderful companionship and the association with her parents, brothers and sister which enriched Rufus Jones's life beyond measure.

Elizabeth brought to her husband a quiet, happy disposition, a delightful sense of humour, a well-trained, disciplined mind, an instinctive gift of doing the right thing at the right time, infinite patience, and a deep religious faith, not expressed in vocal ministry but in everything she did.

Before they were married there had come an offer for service in England. Rufus Jones was asked to become Director of Studies at Woodbrooke, Birmingham, soon to be opened. There was much to attract Rufus Jones to a life in England; proximity to John Wilhelm Rowntree and his plans, a leading rôle in the new settlement, and for his wife a return, in a sense, to a family eager to welcome her and her husband. Rufus and Elizabeth Jones sailed to England in the summer of 1902. John Wilhelm Rowntree, George and Elsie Cadbury, William Charles Braithwaite, and others, presented a strong case for him to accept the Woodbrooke offer.

On the other hand there were his career of service at Haverford College, the editorship of *The American Friend*, and the needs of the Five Years Meeting, which was due to hold its first session that autumn. It took him until November to decide not to go to Woodbrooke, but once decided there were no regrets, and it was a place always especially dear to him. He was happy that Rendel Harris could have the position of Director of Studies. Rufus Jones was invited to give a series of lectures at the Summer School in 1903, preceding the opening of Woodbrooke's first regular term. This was "the most important course I have ever given. It later formed the substance of the book entitled *Social Law in the Spiritual World*, which embodied my philosophy of life up to that time."[35]

Lowell did not come to England with his parents in 1903. He had been ill with diphtheria, but seemed to be entirely well when Rufus and Elizabeth Jones sailed for England. He went with his nurse to Ardonia and his grandparents.

On the voyage, for no apparent reason, Rufus Jones felt

himself invaded with a new sense of God's love. On arrival at Liverpool he found a cable stating that Lowell was very ill. A second cable came almost at once announcing Lowell's death on July 16th.

Lowell's radiant companionship with Rufus Jones had been the most wonderful gift which life had brought. "The dreadful news has almost broken my heart," he wrote to Sallie's stepmother. "No mortal can know what I have suffered these three days. May the dear God help us all."[36]

As Rufus Jones walked along a street in Birmingham he saw a child beating against an iron gate which had swung shut, locking her out. She was sobbing for her mother and, as Rufus Jones watched, the mother did come, unlocked the gate and gathered the frightened, crying child in her arms, "Didn't you know mother would come?"

"Didn't you know God would come?" Suddenly the father saw the parallel in his own situation. Without any doubt, he knew that God was on the other side of the gate, of the closed door. God would open the door and understand the suffering; even more, God suffered, too.

Friends at Woodbrooke were overwhelmingly kind. George and Elsie Cadbury took the stricken parents into their home and Rufus Jones went ahead with the lecture course prepared for the Summer School.

GOING FORWARD

In Rufus Jones's life Lowell's death marked the end of youth and preparation. Marriage to Elizabeth Cadbury began a new period of maturity, achievement, and the rich growth into full harvest. The birth of their daughter, Mary Hoxie, on July 27th, 1904, brought a new joy into the home and in September, Rufus and Elizabeth Jones moved into the house on 2 College Circle which they occupied for the rest of their lives.

In 1905 John Wilhelm and Constance Rowntree started for America and on the voyage he became ill with pneumonia. When Rufus Jones met the steamer in New York, John Wilhelm was delirious and did not recognize his friend. He was removed by ambulance to a New York hospital and died on March 9th. He was buried in the Friends' graveyard adjoining the Haverford Meeting House.

Once again Rufus Jones's bright hopes were shattered and he had to go forward under the burden of suffering. Later that year he went to England to deliver a Summer School lecture course which was published in book form, *The Double Search*, God's search for man and man's for God.

He describes in *The Middle Years* his meeting with John Wilhelm Rowntree's father, brother Seebohm and cousin Joshua, and with his friends including William Charles Braithwaite, Joan Mary Fry, and A. Neave Brayshaw at Scalby in John Wilhelm's new library. Here the group began to plan the continuation of the histories so sadly interrupted by death.

"It was decided to merge my projected studies in mysticism with the plan for a history of Quakerism. The completed series of volumes was to cover the history of the mystical-spiritual movements which prepared the way for the birth of Quakerism in the seventeenth century and to tell the story of its rise and its development up to the present century. I was asked to be the editor of this Historical Series, and it was arranged for William Charles Braithwaite to deal with the beginnings and early periods of Quakerism and for me to write the background movements and the history of Quakerism from 1725 onward, both in England and America. I consequently returned home that summer with a project of added literary labour which was to occupy the next sixteen years of my life."[37] The mystical library collected by John Wilhelm Rowntree was at his disposal. Financially the way was eased by the newly-formed Joseph Rowntree Charitable Trust which enabled Rufus Jones to get books and secretarial help.

He read nearly every Quaker Journal and the minutes of many Meetings. He asked many Friends to help, both in the United States and elsewhere, and there was endless research. Tuesdays and Thursdays were kept free from classes and in those mornings he shut himself up in his study to be disturbed only for emergency calls. There was, however, a midweek meeting for the Haverford students on three Thursday mornings in the month to which every student was required to come, and Rufus Jones always, if possible, attended these. Speaking to that group of young men meant that he went to meeting having spent some time beforehand getting his "heart and mind prepared," as the beautiful query recommends. He found time to sit quietly, drawing on the invisible springs of the spirit, storing his mind with the increasing wealth of his knowledge, and communing with God.

He wrote all his books with a pen, never by dictation or with a typewriter. When the galley proofs came from the publishers Elizabeth Jones corrected the proofs carefully, checking also her husband's spelling, which was a bit casual. She investigated every quotation to find the exact wording, and every statement that seemed wide of the mark. Next came the page proof, and when that was corrected, she began on the index. This also served as a triple-check on the proof reading.

Henry Joel Cadbury who, for some years lived near by, often shared this task with her, as indeed, did Rufus Jones who read everything, too. Henry Cadbury was an invaluable help and had an eagle eye for errors. What a trio this was, husband, wife and brother working together in superb partnership, with joy in the doing.

William Charles Braithwaite and A. Neave Brayshaw were his constant correspondents during these years. Their handwriting was beautiful to see, but difficult to read. When letters arrived they would be laid aside for a free evening and Elizabeth Jones would read them aloud. She could decipher every word but Rufus Jones did not even try.

Rufus Jones found his college work full of interest and joy though he found little to be joyful about yet as far as his impact on American Quakerism was concerned.

In February 1907 his article, "Divine Presence in Human Life," was published in the *Friends Fellowship Papers* and

George Newman in the April issue of *Friends Quarterly Examiner* referred enthusiastically to Rufus Jones's interpretation of the Inner Light in the above article and in his book *Social Law in the Spiritual World*, an interpretation which many Friends had failed to understand or approve.

"Early Friends," George Newman wrote, "thought of the Inward Light as 'a principle of God's nature *but not of man's nature*,' as Isaac Penington put it. Now it seems to us that Rufus Jones . . . has made clear, once and for all, the conception that 'the Inner Light, the true seed, is no foreign substance added to an undivine human life . . . ,' " but that we are called, he concluded, to "a clear utterance and an evident practice of the great verities of personal contact with the Truth, of an indwelling divinity and of that inward life, not as a foreign or external or supernatural thing, but as an inherent and elemental part of our being." [38]

Rufus Jones replied to George Newman in May, "I am very thankful for thy editorial. I was beginning to wonder whether there was any use trying to bring any larger points of view to the notice of Friends. All my attempts seemed to fall so flat that I questioned whether I was not wasting my time and ink! The studies on 'Inner Light' in *Social Law* [have] been left largely to the oblivion of silence. This recent study, 'Divine Presence in Human Life,' which I felt was the most important chapter I had yet written, was receiving a slender, nagging sort of comment which quite depressed me. Thy study of it was the first word I had had which indicated an appreciation of its significance. It did me good 'all over' to find that there was at least one person who knew what I was doing. I will go on now and take a new lease of life." [39]

Another sabbatical year, in 1908, made it possible for him and his family to come to England for several months. They took a house in Charlbury in the early spring and Rufus Jones travelled daily to Oxford where he worked in the Bodleian Library. At London Yearly Meeting he gave the first Swarthmore Lecture, entitled *Quakerism a Religion of Life*, and he

entered fully into British Quaker affairs.   Ties of friendship
were strengthened.

There was a trip to Switzerland that summer which included Henry J. Cadbury and John Wilhelm Rowntree's widow
and children.   Returning one evening to Grindelwald, after
climbing the Faulhorn, Constance Rowntree rushed her children to the balcony of the hotel, while Rufus Jones snatched
his child from bed and together they saw a double rainbow
span the entire valley.   It may have seemed a useless effort,
for the youngest two in the group were only three and four
years old, but the parents hoped that somehow the children
might share in the majestic beauty of that moment.   Years
later, these children grown into women and dear friends, discovered that they all counted that moment of the double
rainbow an earliest memory, a flash of beauty from which
they dated their beginnings as conscious individuals.

By 1909 the first volume in the Rowntree Series of Quaker
Histories, *Studies in Mystical Religion,* was published.   Two
years later appeared *Quakers in the American Colonies* the author-
ship of which Rufus Jones shared with Isaac Sharpless and
Amelia Mott Gummere.   He also published his first book for
children, *Hebrew Heroes.*   Everywhere he went children came
to thank him for writing this book of stories for them.   Friend-
ships with boys and girls were an integral part of his life.

During the summer of 1911 the family went to Marburg,
Germany where they lived in a twelfth century house under
the shadow of the castle.   Rufus Jones worked with Theodor
Sippel, scholar and authority on mysticism, whose friendship
and help through the years he deeply prized.   Elizabeth with
her excellent German, spent many hours reading material,
and together these three prepared another volume in the Series,
Spiritual Reformers in the 16th and 17th Centuries.

October 1912 brought the third gathering of the Five Years
Meeting, held in Indianapolis, Indiana.   A group of British
Friends attended.   A month earlier, there was a trip to the
Canadian Rockies with George Newman and Arnold S. Rown-
tree who were studying prospects in Canada for the migration

of adult school men with their families. This year Rufus
Jones retired from the editorship of *The American Friend*.

It was obvious, however, that he could not be entirely
happy without a paper to edit! A year later when he was in
England again, it was decided to transform the *British Friend*
into an American-British periodical under his editorship, to
be called *Present Day Papers*, a *Monthly Journal for the Presentation of Vital and Spiritual Christianity*. It was edited at Haverford and appeared from January 1914 until December 1915
when the war made it difficult to carry on an international
journal. This Monthly "has the roots of its life very deep
in the past. It is an instance of an old life in a new form and
in a strange land. The *British Friend* has merged its independent life into the new enterprise and the memorable *Present
Day Papers* of 1898–1902 edited by our beloved John Wilhelm
Rowntree, is revived in name at least.''[40]

LIGHTS ARE GOING OUT

Shortly before leaving England in 1913, Rufus Jones spent
a few days in Anglesey with George Newman and his wife,
Arnold Rowntree, William Charles Braithwaite and others.
During the dark years of war which followed, his mind turned
to the gaiety and laughter he had enjoyed with these English
Friends, and the visit, which, in the last year of peace, seemed
to crown the rich association of nearly thirty years.

Rufus Jones was fifty years old in 1913 and the fact depressed him. Old age seemed near and might prevent him
from carrying out all the schemes he had in mind. The future
appeared as a time of mental decline and physical decay.
That he had achieved more than most people was of no comfort to him. But he had been led to a task from which he
could not turn aside.

When war was declared in August 1914 he was spending a
holiday in the White Mountains of New Hampshire. In the
beauty of this mountain retreat the horror of the war's meaning struck into his soul for he loved people in both Germany
and England.

He wrote in September: "Beneath all overt acts and decisions the immense subconscious forces, charged with emotion, have been slowly pushing toward this event. There
are no words which can express the gravity of the tragedy.
It is one of those appalling events which test to the bottom
our central faith in God, in human goodness, in cosmic rationality and in onward progress. But we must not let our
cable slip in this storm. The supreme faiths of humanity
have always had their births and their baptisms in baffling
mysteries and in the deeps of tragedy and suffering. . . . We
shall come out of this crucible with a new and finer temper
at the heart of our faith. . . . Out of this very flood that seems
to mock at ideals of peace and brotherhood new forces will
appear."[41]

"Whatever may be the 'causes' that have led to this cata-
clysm, our main problems just now must be: How to keep
our faith in God and in the coming of His Kingdom; how to
interpret our ideals of love and peace; how to suffer patiently
and loyally where our ideals collide with systems and requirements that are 'survivals' from the past."[42]

On the day before Christmas 1914 Rufus Jones slipped on
the ice, and struck the back of his head, causing concussion.
Then began a long battle with illness. The doctor encouraged
him to take a sea voyage and early in 1915 he went alone to
Nassau in the Bahamas. The ship sailed into a hurricane and
for several days there was doubt whether it could survive.
On top of the fall, this experience brought him into a nervous
breakdown and he returned from Nassau physically and spiritually exhausted. He managed, with difficulty, to continue
his teaching, but he gave up all outside activities. Speaking
in Meeting he found quite impossible. He tried various cures
but nothing helped and it began to look as though the cloud
would never lift.

Patiently, lovingly, his dear Elizabeth coped with this
visitation. Never hurried, never cross, she went ahead trying
to minister to the varied needs of a sick husband and a growing,

often fretful child, endeavouring to be all things to two very different individuals.

Then they were led to spend a month on Mt. Desert Island, off the Maine coast, where it was hoped that he might begin to come back to his former self. The arrival in July was not promising; a fog covered the island, as heavy and smothering as that which weighed upon his own spirits.

"Unusual outside weather is only one of our many means of discipline. Much harder is the fight with inside weather and more dreary and pitiless are the fogs and east winds of our human spirits. . . . It is not so easy to arm oneself against drizzling moods and drenching tempers within our own interior zones. . . . The fight with stubborn inward weather, the battle with the devil in us, if you will, is the best kind of fighting there is to be done, and he who has conquered conditions of inner climate has now the best victories which crown men. Not least [is] the further discovery—joyous like that of Columbus sighting a new world—that there are inexhaustible resources of divine grace for those who are resolved to rise above the fog and mist, the sleet and snow of dreary inward weather."[43]

Here on Mount Desert Island a schoolmaster, who loved wood-chopping, was staying at the same hotel, and he was blazing new trails on the mountain slopes of the island. Rufus Jones borrowed an axe and joined in the trail blazing, slowly but surely clearing a new trail for himself as his strength returned. It was one of those wonderful coincidences so fruitful of results in his life.

"I have had the rare good fortune to meet during my holidays this summer a real trail-maker. . . . He has been taking me along as a companion of his walks and as a helper in the work. . . . What we are finding is that any old trail needs a good deal of restoration work done upon it . . . and must be re-marked so that the wayfarer cannot miss the trail." In the course of their work they found that a "disastrous forest fire had swept over that region and had blasted the entire mountain side. . . . Nature was, however, doing her best to repair the injury. A green carpet of new blueberry bushes covered the whole region where the fire had gone and the soil was already pushing into life the buried seeds that held in their germs a new forest for a new generation. . . .

"It is happy work to go out in this tonic air, on these granite hills . . . and to cut trails and mark paths for future feet to fresh scenes of beauty and to new sources of physical health and vitality. But it is not so easy to discover how to make those other trails which guide the soul of man to new sources of life and power. Before our eyes we see the blasting fire moving across the old world. . . . As soon as *life* gets a chance to work again, it will, in its own way, repair the damage and havoc. . . . What will be needed most will be the trail-makers, with solid cairns and clear-pointing arrows, to help the souls of men to discover the true way of life and the real sources of spiritual power."[44]

Dr. Francis G. Peabody, his friend from Harvard days, invited him to preach one Sunday at the Northeast Harbour Union Church, across the island. At this prospect, his illness returned; he could not undertake to speak to that select congregation. Dr. Peabody would take no refusal and Rufus Jones went over to see the church and try out his voice in the empty building. His heart sank as the echoes came back to him. Next day, after a sleepless night, he faced a congregation which filled the church. He rose trembling, his knees nearly gave way, but his voice came out clear and unshaken. He preached a great sermon, so his friends who gathered around him afterwards told him, and he knew that his lost powers had returned. That moment marked the end of his illness and Rufus Jones began to live again. He returned to his work at Haverford with a new vitality and he tapped new resources.

As a boy in the Providence School, Rufus Jones had weathered a severe test to his faith in God when he had to choose between the Genesis story of creation and the scientific facts. A wise and deeply religious teacher had made it possible for him to see that one could believe both in facts and in

God. This teacher, Thomas Battey, "courageously and fear-lessly faced the facts of science as they broke upon the world in the nineteenth century, and he not only kept his own faith, but he led his students on into a deeper faith than they had before they came to school."[45] When both Sallie and Lowell were taken from him, these experiences might again have closed the door forever between him and God, but they served to make more obvious than ever that "underneath are the everlasting arms."

His illness and the war brought new tests to Rufus Jones's faith. God seemed to him to be destroying His world and, for a time, to have forsaken it. Rufus Jones had tried to be an optimist, believing that life was slowly moving upward, and was a spiral, not a circle. In the years before the war, although there had been many slips back, it was fairly easy to believe that the steps forward were greater than those backward. Men were ready to

> Move upward, working out the beast,
> And let the ape and tiger die. . . .
> And hear at times a sentinel
> Who moves about from place to place,
> And whispers to the worlds of space
> In the deep night, that all is well.[46]

But now all was far from well, and Rufus Jones, like many another had to find a new faith for this new age. For many, faith was never recovered, and life became a "Wasteland." But for him the lines from Goethe's *Faust* which he quoted often, must have brought him the answer for which he longed.

> Thou hast it destroyed,
> The beautiful world,
> With powerful fist:
> In ruin 'tis hurled,
> By the blow of a demigod shattered!
> The scattered
> Fragments into the Void we carry

Deploring
The beauty perished beyond restoring.
Mightier
For the children of men,
Brightlier
Build it again,
In thine own bosom build it anew![47]

That was it! With God's help, man could rebuild the broken world. It was man's blindness which had destroyed it. God needed men with vision and dedication to "build Jerusalem in England's green and pleasant land,"[48] and in France and in Germany. The war laid a new responsibility upon young men and women all over the world. "Now, God be thanked Who has matched us with His hour."[49]

The Burden of the World's Suffering

The American Friends Service Committee came into existence on April 30th, 1917, only three weeks after the United States entered the war. Rufus Jones could not attend the first meeting but the group which met together that day asked him to be chairman of the new committee. He agreed to accept this position, providing it did not demand too much of his time, for his teaching schedule was heavy and he was hard at work on the sixth and last volume of the Rowntree Series, *Later Periods of Quakerism*. The condition of his acceptance is amusing for there was hardly a day for many years when he was not involved in some service for the A.F.S.C.[50] He was on constant call for trips to Washington or New York, for committees in Philadelphia which might last all day and into the night. Yet he never slighted his Haverford students nor slackened his work on *Later Periods*.

His introduction to *A Service of Love in War Time*, the story of the A.F.S.C., tells something about the author himself and much about the underlying reasons for the committee's birth.

"This book . . . is the interpretation of a way of life. The relief work took on a peculiar form and character just because it was the expression of a definite religious faith and sprang naturally out of an inner spirit and attitude to life. . . . [Friends took their unique and difficult position] because they were inwardly pledged to a way of life which, if extended through the world, would eliminate the seeds of war and would bring new and higher forces into operation within the fabric of society. They could not, therefore, of a sudden change the faith of a lifetime and substitute the methods of war for the slower but not less effective forces of love and co-operation. . . . This position was no hasty expedient; it was as deep as life itself. . . .

"The one impossible course for those of us who held this faith was to refuse the call to fight and at the same time to refuse all responsibility for the tragedy . . . [to] assume for ourselves a holier attainment than that possessed by other Christians. . . . No, to do that was to lose the soul. . . . We were all in our degree to blame [for] the agony of which in some measure we were all bound to bear a share. . . . We wanted to show our faith in action . . . in a way that would both bring healing to the awful wounds of war and at the same time take us out of self and selfish aims and carry us into the furnace where others were suffering. . . . Now that hunger and disease and greed and post-war hate have revealed their . . . malevolent sway, possibly it may be a relief to turn away from the dark picture and to read the simple story of an attempt to practice love both with friends and enemies in the midst of the disaster and catastrophe."[51]

The success of the A.F.S.C. in living to some extent up to these great words of its chairman has been in a large measure due to the indomitable belief that love does work.

He was particularly pleased that the A.F.S.C. brought British and American Friends into a close, working relationship. The complicated arrangement whereby A.F.S.C. was a co-worker with the Friends War Victims Relief Committee of London and, at the same time, an arm of the American Red Cross was certainly difficult, but the A.F.S.C. could never have done what it did if the "War-Vics" had not made this co-operation possible.

Rufus Jones sailed for France shortly before Christmas in 1918. He visited the workers and tried to interpret British and Americans to one another. He let them see the vision that he had for the great service they were rendering and he told them that differences of viewpoints regarding food or sense of humour must not prevent their getting on with their work together. The fact that he shared their frustrations, their hardships, ploughed through the mud, ate their food and wore their uniform, made him one with them.

When the young people came back from the French re-construction work to their homes in the United States, Quakerism had a new meaning for them. They went to France "immature and inarticulate; they are coming back men who have been tested in the fire and are now, as the steel-makers say, 'bloom-furnaced'. . . . They are clarified and deepened in their religious experience."[52]

A year later, Rufus Jones wrote in a letter, "My A.F.S.C. work has been a tremendous load, but it has been greatly worth while. It has done more to unite Quakers in America than anything else ever has or than all other things put to-gether. It has, too, given a new spiritual power to our Quakerism and it has awakened a universal interest in Quaker-ism. All that is in addition to the effect it has had on the field where the service lay. As I look back over the four years during which I have carried the load I am inclined to think it is the most important thing I have ever done. God has been very good to me and in spite of the fact that this has been the heaviest winter's work I have ever done, I am in the best health I ever can remember to have had. I do not understand where the energy comes from."[53]

Serving as chairman or honorary chairman of the A.F.S.C., as Rufus Jones did for most of the years between 1917 and 1948, gave him full opportunity to keep close to the flood tides which were enriching the Society of Friends. He was an excellent chairman of a meeting, bringing in just the right touch of humour at the right moment, easing tensions and guiding discussions so that the important issues were dealt with adequately. He could go through a long, difficult agenda and bring the meeting to a close at the proper time. It is not surprising that he occupied the chair for many organisations.

His own life was well-ordered. He carried on his many and varied obligations without letting them tangle with one another. He had time to spare for at least one game of golf each week or for cutting trees in the college woods. He did his work with a sense of serenity, although it must be said there were occasions when this serenity gave way to confusion and frustration. He concentrated on the occupation of the moment, putting his best into whatever he was doing. Somehow he managed to bring into each occupation the accumulated wealth of past experience while, at the same time, he was preparing for the work which lay ahead. He kept up with the daily newspapers, the Quaker periodicals, the journals of religious thought, philosophy and psychology, and read important current books in addition to his historical research. He never failed to read *Punch* each week, as it came to the Haverford College Library.

CONFERENCE PAN QUAKER

Thus William Charles Braithwaite referred to the All Friends Conference held in London during August 1920. Following this there were also two other conferences, at Oxford and at Jordans, a test for the endurance of Friends. Rufus Jones and his family went to England, their first visit since the war. In addition to all the preparation he had to do for the London Conference, he had written three books—the Swarthmore Lecture, *The Nature and Authority of Conscience*, *The Remnant*, and *A Service of Love in War Time*. The manuscript for the two volumes, *Later Periods of Quakerism*, was nearly finished, and he brought it with him to London for type-setting.

By 1919 he had written to his friend, L. Violet Hodgkin,

"I am reading William Charles Braithwaite's splendid second
volume [*Second Period of Quakerism*, just published]. Now it is
up to me to wind up the series. My volume is practically
done, even the introduction written, but I hope to put the
finishing touches to it next autumn before sending the MS.
to the printers. It seems amazing to think the momentous
task which was rolled upon us in 1905 is so near completion
and that five large volumes are already out. I shall feel very
strange not to be carrying this load and no longer to be under
this immense responsibility. Nobody could have been a
better co-labourer than W.C.B. We have worked most happily together."[54]

But the completion took longer than Rufus Jones expected
and he wrote again to Violet Hodgkin in 1921, "My History
is practically done. We have a little more of the page proof
to read but it should be finished before I sail [for Europe in
May on an A.F.S.C. visit]; the index is nearly done. It is a
book of an even thousand pages. I have had an Atlas's
burden on my poor old back. It is a large and complicated
task but now it is done and I shall not do it again. I hope
nobody will have to do this same sort of thing again!"[55]

A special suitcase contained the precious pages when Rufus
Jones brought this manuscript to London in 1920. The bag
was never out of his sight during the voyage and the family
knew that whatever else had to be sacrificed in case of a
disaster, this must be saved. There was a large label, tied to
the bag's handle, giving name and address, and the sentence,
"*If Lost, Return to Owner*." When the journey was over and
the bag and its contents reached the English publisher without mishap, everyone relaxed.

The high-spot of that summer was neither conference nor
lecture, momentous as they were, but the aftermath, when
the four friends sought relaxation on northern moors.

"How do prophets occupy themselves when not prophesy-
ing? It fell to my happy lot," wrote George Newman, "to
travel at pleasure with a distinguished American Professor of
Philosophy; the English historian of Quakerism [William

Charles Braithwaite]; and a well-known director in a famous firm in the north of England [Arnold S. Rowntree] immediately after the termination of the conference. They had exhausted themselves, and possibly others also. I was selected as a victim of their subsequent reaction. We began our delightful journey through the North Riding moors, the ostensible purpose of all our action and inaction being to supply a rest-cure for the American Professor."

Several days passed. George Newman continued, "I have to report . . . great peace and quietude overcame our cousin [Rufus Jones] and the fascinations of the higher criticism and manifold uncertainties of psychological philosophy gave place to a strange professorial monologue, a contented and fully satisfied sort of murmur . . . respecting the utility of stone walls on moors." The question under consideration was, were these walls built to keep the rabbits in or out? "The stress and density of the situation, gave way to the brief but final answer delivered in Greek Chorus, 'anyhow for rabbits'. . . . This, then, was the Professor's rest-cure. Dear friend and comrade and beloved Professor."[56]

The cure completed, they returned to Low Hall at Scalby to Elizabeth Jones and Mary Hoxie.

Of Perilous Seas and Faery Lands

A sabbatical leave from Haverford College in 1923 made it possible for Rufus and Elizabeth Jones to take a long-planned voyage to Greece and the Holy Land, as a kind of final travel fling. Rufus Jones had reached sixty, not quite as ancient an age as fifty had seemed, but he felt his travelling days were probably coming to an end. They embarked in the *Empress of Scotland* in February, 1923, but under most inauspicious circumstances.

On Thanksgiving Day, 1922—the last Thursday in November—in front of the Cadbury home he was struck by a motor car and hurled several feet. One leg and several ribs were broken and he was still on crutches when he boarded the ship.

In spite of this the voyage was a great success. Augustus

T. Murray and his wife were spending the year in Athens. School and college classmate of Rufus Jones, he met the ship and took the invalid, crutches and all, to the places Rufus Jones wanted to see. He was pushed and pulled up Mars Hill where he read aloud St. Paul's speech on the Unknown God, "Whom therefore ye ignorantly worship, him declare I unto you."[57] The short visit made him determined to come again.

As the ship neared Palestine, Rufus Jones kept his Bible in his hand. Some members of the cruise were surprised at his apparent intimacy with a country he had never seen. One woman remarked, after he had explained that this was due to a life-time of Bible study, "Why I'd have brought a Bible too if I had realised it was about Palestine."

The days in the Holy Land were deeply moving to Rufus Jones as he traced the steps of his great Bible heroes and saw where Jesus had lived and died. The shrines, covering the supposed spots of birth and burial, did not impress him, but the shepherd's field, the well at Nazareth, the olive trees, the stones and the flowers were unchanged. So, too, was the Sea of Galilee with its calm surface or its turbulent waves.

While their party was in a small boat on the lake, a sudden storm arose and the boat, its engine stopped because a rope had caught round the propeller, was being carried to some rocks. One of the boatmen plunged over and untangled the rope. The engine was re-started and the passengers returned somewhat the worse from the rough sea and the anxiety, but unhurt.

Before returning to America they visited England in order for Rufus Jones to do research needed for his book *The Church's Debt to Heretics*. While at Oxford he learned of a remarkable masseuse there, whose skilled though painful treatment on his leg enabled him to walk again as well as ever.

This journey, in spite of his "last voyage" expectations, turned out to be the beginning of new adventures. The Y.M.C.A. planned to hold a conference in northern China in the summer of 1926, celebrating their forty years of work in China. Rufus Jones was invited to be one of the speakers.

"This is our first day on the Pacific," he wrote in his diary on June 25th, 1926, "a new situation, with new noises, new calls. We must meet the unusual and speak to the age, to the eastern mind in fresh and creative ways.

"All seem alike expectant that the journey will be fruitful and that it is a divinely ordered mission. May it indeed be so. In any case, I am starting forth with a rare joy. I have seldom ever been so penetrated with a deep happiness. My dear wife and daughter seem to share it with me."

The family reached Japan early in July where they spent a fortnight crowded with beautiful scenes and interesting experiences. Taking a small Japanese boat from Kobe they sailed through the Inland Sea to the Chinese seaport, Tsingtao. In a nearby summer resort Elizabeth Jones and Mary Hoxie remained for a month with Y.M.C.A. friends, while Rufus Jones went to the important conference held in Tsinan. The heat during this period was worse than anything he had ever known. A retreat on Tai Shan, Confucius' sacred mountain, followed immediately after the Tsinan conference, when a small group of Chinese and foreign leaders met together. Henry T. Hodgkin was with Rufus Jones during these days, adding greatly to his enjoyment.

There were many risks to health on this Chinese trip. Outbreaks of cholera occurred in several places and there was reason enough to fear what effect a twenty-two course feast might have, but he threw aside his fears and enjoyed everything without ill effects, although he had been on a restricted diet for years.

At the end of his time in China he wrote in his diary, October 29th, "[Canton] was a splendid finish of my three months in China. In all I had 115 meetings and conferences, nearly all of them marked by serious attention and decided sympathy. I am filled with thanksgiving to God for inspiration, guidance and strength. I came to the end of the wonderful days with hush and awe."

Rufus Jones and his family sailed for Ceylon and India,

stopping for a few days in Manila. The supreme moment of the month was a visit to Gandhi at his Ashram in Sabarmarti, a few miles from Ahmedabad. He closed a long entry in his diary, December 1st, describing Gandhi and their conversation together, with this comment, "Gandhi's simplicity is as natural as everything else about his life. There is no pose in his nature. He is thoroughly unspoiled and the most satisfactory thing about my visit was the conviction I brought away that here was a man who had attracted the attention of the whole world, a man who had controlled the thought of millions and influenced the destiny of an empire and who yet was still sincere and simple and unspoiled. It is the last test of greatness and nobility of soul."

Christmas week was spent at the Friends Schools in Ramallah, near Jerusalem, and after brief stops in Vienna and London, the family returned to Haverford.

The rich summer and autumn spent in the Orient, the interest and appreciation from people in cultures completely different from his own, were wonderful experiences.

He had little sense of his own importance and he was never spoiled or made blasé by the acclaim people gave to him. It was pleasant to know that men and women of all ages, cultures, religions and walks of life found his message answering their needs. But there was a deeper satisfaction than that, and it was the knowledge that he was fulfilling what God wanted him to do. He was living out the prophecies spoken by Aunt Peace and James Rhoads.

In 1929 there was another family trip to England, Greece, Italy and Sicily with brief visits to Geneva and Paris, and then in 1932 came the second visit to the Orient. The Laymen's Mission Inquiry Commission, with headquarters in New York City, invited Rufus Jones to be a member of a group to evaluate a previous study made of mission work in India, Ceylon, Burma, China, Korea, and Japan. The first group of Fact Finders, often humorously called the "fault finders," had done its work during 1930–1931 and the second group started in the late summer of 1931. Rufus Jones could not undertake the entire survey; he and his family joined the Commission in Hong Kong by the first of February 1932, about ten days after the Japanese had attacked Shanghai. The *President Grant* did however sail up the Yangtze and anchor overnight in the river at Shanghai, and left again without mishap. Japanese planes were seen flying overhead; the few visitors who came on board while the ship lay at anchor gave a distressing account of what was happening. It looked as though the Commission's work could not continue in China.

Rufus Jones met his colleagues at Hong Kong, as they arrived from India and Burma; they were able to complete their study in South China during the month of February and by the time they were ready to go north the fighting had stopped. The war did not prevent their work and they were able to visit the areas previously included on the itinerary. In April the Commission reached Nara, Japan, where they spent a week working on the China report, and during May the survey continued in Japan. The Commission stopped for two weeks in Honolulu to begin their final report, entitled *Re-Thinking Missions*. Later in the summer the group gathered together again in Rockland, Maine, to complete the book.

Rufus Jones wrote two of the chapters and helped considerably in the editing of all the material, a task he shared with Dr. William Ernest Hocking of Harvard University, the chairman of the Commission. There were so many facts and points of view to be correlated that it seemed, at times, to be quite impossible to include the necessary information and to resolve the conflicting interpretations. Rufus Jones, with his unfailing sense of right and order, his clear and direct mind, his gift of humour when tensions were strong, helped to produce a book which everyone in the group approved.

These two visits to the Orient put great demands upon his strength but he met them magnificently, and enjoyed his tasks as well as absorbing the wonder of his surroundings.

THE BEST IS YET TO BE

The retiring age for members of the faculty at Haverford College, as in most American institutions, is sixty-five. Rufus Jones reached this age in 1928, but his uneasy premonitions about being old, which had clouded his fiftieth birthday, had somehow disappeared! The college asked him to continue his teaching and he was delighted to accept the opportunity.

Haverford College celebrated its centennial in October 1933. Rufus Jones wrote for this occasion, *Haverford College, A History*, and made up his mind to retire in June 1934. Although he had been urged to continue a while longer, after all he was only seventy, he was quite adamant. He was determined to stop his work before the college authorities reached the point of wishing that he would.

There is a humorous college song about "old Founder's bell is ringing." But the ringing of Founder's bell is not always a matter to laugh about. It had, for forty years, called Rufus Jones across the Cricket Circle from his home to his class-room. He realised that he wanted to be out of ear-shot of Founder's bell when the autumn semester began in 1934. He and his wife sailed for England and, after some travels in Europe, returned to Haverford early in 1935, by which time he was adjusted to the fact that he was no longer teaching students at the college.

Retirement meant that there was more time for him to spend on work he loved. There was the Service Committee; there was his writing; there were more and more invitations to preach at college and university chapels. On his return home from these Rufus Jones would report that every seat was filled and that he had found the students most responsive. He kept on 'lighting candles' for young and old but he had a special gift for reaching the minds of college students.

He had much to do in preparation for the second Friends World Conference in 1937. He was asked to be its presiding chairman, a post which he was well fitted to hold, but which he did not enthusiastically accept. All summer long he lived in dread of the responsibility, and he became troubled in his mind. A disturbing roaring in his ears developed. He was assured by physicians, however, that there was no need for worry or to fear an injury to the brain. He gradually over-came this fear and learned to accept the buzzing, which never quite left him.

When September arrived, the time for the All Friends Con-ference, in spite of the heat and the strain he carried his responsibilities as chairman with his usual vigour and en-thusiasm.

Early in 1938 Rufus and Elizabeth Jones sailed for South Africa at the invitation of South African Friends and the encouragement of the A.F.S.C. He had his seventy-fifth birthday shortly before his departure and both he and his wife went off to the unknown continent in great spirits. The long sea voyage gave him the kind of holiday he loved. The days in South Africa were full of new contacts and new ex-periences. He lectured in many colleges and saw his friend, Jan Smuts, with whom he had an interesting talk about South Africa and world affairs.

Both Rufus and Elizabeth Jones brought courage and in-spiration to the small groups of Friends as they visited in Quaker homes and attended the General Meeting held, that year, in Port Elizabeth. The journey back to America took them to Madagascar, Singapore and Shanghai.

Events in Europe made settling down at home impossible for him. On the "Day of Broken Glass," in Germany on November 10th, 1938, Jewish shops and synagogues were vandalised. Together with Robert Yarnall and George Wal-ton, Rufus Jones sailed at the end of November for Germany, ready to interview Hitler himself, if need be, in the effort to bring help and comfort to the Jewish people in their suffering.

Rufus Jones had a favourite text, "The Lamb made war on the Beast and overcame him." He believed firmly that the chequer-board of life had a white background on which the black squares were imprinted. On his momentous visit to the

Gestapo headquarters, when the closed door of evil seemed to
open a tiny crack for the admission of love and goodwill,
Rufus Jones believed that the Lamb could and would, eventually conquer the Beast. He felt that the hard men of the
Gestapo were touched for a moment and that in the depths
of their hearts they knew the meaning of *agapé*, a pure, un-
selfish love.

It is questionable, however, whether the visit had any influence at all. The Gestapo promised them that certain of
their requests would be granted and Rufus Jones tried to convince himself that they were. Certainly it was one of the
most difficult experiences the three men had ever had.

In 1914, when the war came, Rufus Jones thought he was
getting old. But in 1939, when all the forces of hate were
again unleashed, there was not quite the same despair which
had clouded him before. He was now an old man and he
had to sit by and watch, an unhappy spectator, suffering over
this tragedy. In spite of his sorrow, he was able to keep his
optimism and his zest for each day. Young and old who
turned to him found him alert and alive.

In Dulce Jubilo

The house at 2 College Circle, Haverford, looked out over
the cricket field, to the mighty oaks and maples. When
leaves were gone in autumn and winter, the college buildings
were visible. Everything about Haverford was deeply
satisfying.

There was a fourth member of the College Circle household, Ada Smith, who came in 1905 to be cook general, and
nursemaid for Mary Hoxie, and who remained as family
friend until the house was closed in June 1953. Ada's parents
had been slaves until Abraham Lincoln's Emancipation Proclamation, but Ada, next to youngest in a family of sixteen
children, had been born free. She could neither read nor
write, but she was a person of passionate loyalty and deep
religious faith. She gave everything she had to her beloved

"Mr. and Mrs. Jones and her Miss Mary." She knew her "Mr. Jones" was a great man and she did everything possible to make his life comfortable. It was to Ada that Rufus Jones said his last farewell before leaving the house on a trip and to Ada that he gave his first joyous shout of greeting when he returned.

Haverford was home. Yet in the spring his mind began turning again to South China, Maine. He had been spending short vacations there ever since his school days. The old house built by Grandfather Abel belonged to him, although his brother Herbert and family occupied it. There was a twenty-five acre field a mile away, adjoining his Cousin Richard Jones's summer home. As a boy he had, in winter, coasted from the top of the hill on this land, sliding at terrific speed down the slope and across the ice on the lake. He had decided then that this was an ideal location for a house and in 1915 the owner was willing to sell Rufus Jones the field he wanted. During the Christmas holidays he and his brother Herbert cut trees in the woodlot and drew the plans for a summer cottage. The house was ready for the family to occupy by July 1916.

He named this home Pendle Hill after the Pendle Hill in Lancashire which George Fox climbed with "much ado, it was so steep." Sitting on his Pendle Hill porch, Rufus Jones saw the lake spread out before him; the shores with their beautiful white birches and dark green pine trees; the hills and, in the far distance, a range of mountains. He watched the sunsets and their transformation of the lake into sheets of gold and crimson; the storms which swept over the lake in a fury of wind and rain. He loved the days of greater visibility when the distant mountains were clear and blue, a northwest day which seemed to bring the horizon very close. On other days the mountains were hidden in haze.

There was a satisfaction here unlike anything he had ever known. It was a mingling of self with beauty, and it was not so much that this cottage and field belonged to him but that he belonged to them. They fitted and had found each other.

His summers were not all idleness, by any means.   He
worked at his desk every morning and wrote many of his
books and lectures in the Pendle Hill study, and later in the
little log cabin he had built away from the cottage.   Un-
troubled here by telephone or conversation he wrote, looking
out over the lake as he paused for the right word.   In the
afternoons he swam in the lake and hoed in his vegetable
garden and he found time to read a great number of books
during the weeks at South China.

The Fourth of July celebration of Independence Day was a
high point for everyone, with a picnic and stories told by
"Cousin Rufus."   The favourite story, which he had learned
from William Charles Braithwaite, was of Brother Jucundus,
the monk from St. Mary's Abbey in York, who was a model
Brother for 364 days in the year but on Lady's Day slipped
away from the Abbey to York Fair.   Here temptations beset
him and he could not refuse.   Getting thoroughly drunk,
Brother Jucundus would clamber into a swing-boat and shout
at the top of his lungs, "In dulce jubilo! Up, *Up*, Up we go!"
For this serious offence poor Brother Jucundus was taken
down to the Abbey cellar and walled in, with a jug of water,
a loaf of bread, and, to bring the Middle Ages closer to the
Twentieth Century, an electric toaster was included.   How
Brother Jucundus weathered this desperate punishment and
ended the tale as an Abbot, Rufus Jones gave with tremendous
flourishes, bringing in as often as he could the magic refrain,
"In dulce jubilo! Up, *Up*, Up we go!"   If he varied so much
as a jot or tittle in the telling, a child would instantly demand the correct version.   Sleepy children went home across
the fields chanting "In dulce jubilo" as they went, not knowing the meaning of the words, but feeling the happiness of
the moment.

These summers at South China were the "more yet" of
life.   It was his childhood association with the bleak, unhappy times forgotten and the happy memories added to the
joys of the present.   His Maine heritage was precious to him
and it was good to touch base for a period each year.   But,

at the end of the summer, when his potatoes were dug and put in a barrel, his writing stint was finished and his books read, he was ready to go back to Haverford, to go home. He was rested and restored and eager for the winter's work.

A Garden Greater than Eden

When in April 1943 Rufus Jones went to Cambridge, Massachusetts, to give the Ingersoll Lecture at Harvard University, on "The Spell of Immortality" he was much under the weight of this undertaking. Rufus Jones gave his lecture not knowing that his dear Elizabeth had been taken suddenly ill with a coronary thrombosis. But as soon as the lecture was over, he was told. Once more he felt the shadow of death. But Elizabeth Jones took this illness as she had everything else, calmly and serenely. She was an excellent patient and settled quietly into the process of recovery. She learned to find pleasure in small recreations which did not tax her strength, but her husband had little use for the crossword puzzles and detective stories with which she passed long hours. He felt sad that his wife who had worked with him in the Bodleian Library and the British Museum, should allow her excellent mind to drop to so low an order of mental stimulants! He took many a trip, however, to the Haverford Library just for the sake of hunting up a crossword and he managed to wrest a good deal of enjoyment from this form of research, though he would never admit it.

By October of 1943 Elizabeth Jones was entirely well and able to participate again in some of her many activities. But she realised that the time had come to take life more slowly and she resigned from many of her committees. It was impossible to believe that she was then seventy-two years of age for she seemed young in her outlook and interests. She radiated serenity and happiness and her face showed no lines.

Rufus Jones was the grand elder statesman, not only in the Society of Friends, but also in a wider religious field. His radiant face caught attention wherever he went, and there was a contagion of enthusiasm about him which permeated the room he entered or even the train he travelled on. He was a man alive in every fibre of his heart and mind and body. But he was eighty years old. People marvelled at this couple who lived as though they were in middle years of activity.

The year 1945 brought to an end the separation of New England Yearly Meeting into two bodies which had taken place in 1845 over the Gurney-Wilbur controversy. It had taken one hundred years to heal this breach and Friends gathered together in the sessions of the united Yearly Meeting under a deep sense of thanksgiving. It was for Rufus Jones a great moment.

Later in that year he attended the sessions of The Five Years Meeting in Richmond, Indiana, and held, as he had since 1912, the post of chairman for the Business Committee. He gave the opening lecture at the Five Years Meeting, entitled *Original Quakerism, a Movement not a Sect*. "Whether a Movement is to have its day and be 'done away' depends on the expansive scope and interior depth of its seed principle, its capacity to go on vitalising lives. . . . It is to that high hope and expectation that I call you [that Friends were to be a seed and germ of essential Christianity for the whole world]. We can if we will, set our sails to the divine breezes and move away from the shallow waters out into the deeps to which God calls us."[58]

During 1947 Rufus Jones was not quite so vigorous or quite so well, but he kept going at a fairly strenuous pace. He could not bear to give up his engagements, and strength always seemed to be given him for them. He was engaged to lecture in March 1948 at Union Theological Seminary, New York City, and although it was an effort, he undertook it. He never could refuse anything to do with students. A few days later at the Board Meeting of Bryn Mawr College Trustees he found that the dinner was held in his honour, celebrating his service on the Board for fifty years. This was his last public function. On Sunday he came to Haverford

Meeting and preached with his usual power, but he was not well. Many Friends expressed concern about his health.

He was taken seriously ill that night with a coronary occlusion. Several weeks in the hospital seemed to start him on the way to recovery but he had a second and more severe attack four weeks after the first. For three days he was desperately ill; the family doctor sat up all one night with him and the heart specialist said only a miracle could save him. The miracle occurred. On the third morning the nurse asked Rufus Jones what kind of a night he had had and his voice rang out, with some of its old vigour, "Splendid!"

Rufus Jones had written to Sallie Coutant from Paris in July 1887, "It is my great wish exceeding all others that I may feel in the last hours of my life that I have done my work and that the Great Father is satisfied with my life, so that death may be to me like falling asleep as it is for all who faithfully walk the right road."[59]

He had promised to review a book about Emanuel Swedenborg. It took all his strength to evaluate this long, heavy volume, but he wrote that review, moving his pen slowly and painfully across the pages. He had been asked to give the opening address at New England Yearly Meeting in June. He hoped, for a while that he would be well enough to go, and then even though he could not take his body to the sessions he still had the message in his mind. Slowly he wrote what he wanted to say to his Yearly Meeting, a page each day until he completed *A New Instalment of the Heroic Spirit*, for his daughter to read in his place.

A Call to What is Vital had gone to the publishers before his illness; he and Elizabeth Jones were back at their old task of proof-reading, his bed was strewn with the pages of galley proof just as his study had been for the past forty years and more. He read a little each day, marking the corrections and talking them over with her, showing that his mind was as keen as ever. There were no detective stories nor crossword puzzles for him. The body might fail, but his mind must hold on to the end.

1948

On the morning of June 16th Rufus Jones received from his
stenographer the typed copy of his Yearly Meeting address.
He made a few corrections and laid it aside for his daughter
to read aloud to him so that he might hear how it would
sound as she read it to his friends a few days later. Picking
up the last pages of the galley proof, he read these through
and laid them down. His work was finished. After his
lunch he took a nap, as he always had, and in his sleep he
crossed over from the world that is seen to the one which is
unseen.

Haverford Meeting House was filled and many great things
were said about this dear man who had no enemies but a
host of friends who loved him. His body was laid to rest
in the little graveyard, John Wilhelm Rowntree's grave at
his head, Isaac Sharpless' at his feet. Not long after this a
little girl tried to comfort her brother when an older brother
died. "He won't be lonely in Heaven. You see, Cousin
Rufus is there too!"

Elizabeth Jones lived on quietly in the Haverford home
until 1952. The day of her death, October 26th, was warm
and beautiful and the leaves lay thick on the ground. Two
days later heavy clouds darkened the sky as friends and
family gathered at the Meeting House. But as the little
group turned to leave the grave where she had been placed
beside her husband, the clouds broke away and the autumn
sunset flamed over the western sky. There could be no sad-
ness but only thanksgiving for these two lives.

"If God is GOD, which means in other words, Spirit, Life
of our lives, Love at the heart of things, the over-arching,
under-girding Source of all that is eternally Real and True
and Beautiful and Good, then we already have a two-storied
universe with a Home in it for all we love and a Garden in it
greater than Eden, where transplanted human worth *will*
bloom to profit otherwhere. This faith at least may 'call
home our hearts to quietness.' "[60]

NOTES

1. *Finding the Trail of Life*, p. 20.
2. Note written by M.H.J. during conversation with R.M.J., May, 1948.
3. *Ibid*, July, 1939.
4. *The Trail of Life in College*, pp. 143–144.
5. *Ibid*, p. 146.
6. *Finding the Trail of Life*, pp. 21–22.
7. Letter from R.M.J. to Sarah H. Coutant, July 25th, 1886.
8. R.M.J. to S.H.C., August 7th, 1886.
9. R.M.J. to S.H.C., September 12th, 1886.
10. R.M.J. to S.H.C., September 20th, 1886.
11. R.M.J. to S.H.C., *Ibid*.
12. *Trail of Life in College*, p. 157.
13. R.M.J. to S.H.C., September 20th, 1886.
14. R.M.J. to S.H.C., October 2nd, 1886.
15. R.M.J. to S.H.C., *Ibid*.
16. *Trail of Life in College*, pp. 159–160.
17. R.M.J. to S.H.C., November 21st, 1886.
18. R.M.J. to S.H.C., March 3rd, 1887.
19. R.M.J. to S.H.C., April 12th, 1887.
20. R.M.J. to S.H.C., May 1st, 1887.
21. *Trail of Life in College*, pp. 166–167.
22. *Ibid*, p. 174.
23. *Ibid*, p. 181.
24. *The Middle Years*, p. 14.
25. *Ibid*, p. 36.
26. *Ibid*, p. 38.
27. *The American Friend*, vol. I, July 19th, 1894. Author's italics.
28. Note taken by M.H.J.
29. *Haverford College, A History and an Interpretation*, pp. 94–95.
30. R.M.J. to S.C.J., June 20th, 1897.
31. *Trail of Life in College*, pp. 191–192.
32. William Wordsworth, "The Prelude."
33. *The Middle Years*, pp. 5–6.
34. Note taken by M.H.J. during conversation with R.M.J., April 1948.
35. *The Middle Years*, p. 84.
36. Letter from R.M.J. to Clementine Coutant, Ardonia, July 19th, 1903.
37. *The Middle Years*, pp. 85–86.
38. *Friends Quarterly Examiner*, April 1907, pp. 155–157.
39. R.M.J. to George Newman, May 1907.
40. *Present Day Papers*, January 1914, Editorial.
41. *Present Day Papers*, Vol. I, No. 9, September 1914, p. 247, Editorial.
42. *Present Day Papers*, Vol. I, No. 12, December 1914, p. 341.
43. *Ibid*, Vol. II, No. 9, September 1915, p. 264, Editorial by R.M.J.
44. *Ibid*, Vol. II, No. 8, August 1915, pp. 234–6, Editorial by R.M.J.
45. Thomas J. Battey, article by R.M.J., July 1931.
46. Alfred, Lord Tennyson, "In Memoriam," cantos cxviii, xccvi.

47. Goethe's *Faust*, translated by Bayard Taylor, Part I, Scene IV.
48. William Blake, "Jerusalem."
49. Rupert Brooke (Sonnet), 1914, I, *Peace*.
50. American Friends Service Committee.
51. *Service of Love in War Time*, Introduction, pp. xiii–xv.
52. *Ibid*, p. 143.
53. R.M.J. to L. Violet Hodgkin, April 17th, 1921.
54. R.M.J. to L.V.H., July 20th, 1919.
55. R.M.J. to L.V.H., April 17th, 1921.
56. *Friends Quarterly Examiner*, No. 216, 10th Month, 1920; *House of the Four Winds*, pp. 335–344, by G.N.
57. Acts xvii, 22–24.
58. *Original Quakerism*, *A Movement not a Sect*, pp. 3, 24.
59. R.M.J. to S.H.C., July 8th, 1887.
60. *The Radiant Life*, by R.M.J., pp. 136–137.

1

Studies in Mystical Religion

Two great tendencies come into prominence in the entire course of religious history,—the tendency, on the one hand, to regard religion as something permanent and unchanging, and on the other hand, the equally fundamental tendency to revivify and reshape religion through fresh and spontaneous experiences. It is natural that both tendencies should appear, for religion is both eternal and temporal—it is the child of permanence and change. No religion can live and be a power in this evolving world unless it changes and adjusts itself to its environment, and no religion can minister to the deepest needs of men unless it reveals permanent and time-transcending Realities.

Religion has many times lost its power because one of its two essential aspects has been ignored and the other aspect has been pushed to an absurd extreme. It will not do to forget or to overlook the advantages of habit, custom, and system —the storage of the gains of the race. The tendency to value what has worked well furthers order and stability, and keeps the future organic with the past. The conserving spirit, like an invisible mortar, binds the ages together and makes possible *one humanity*. It is the very basis of our social morality and the ground of all our corporate activities.

But, on the other hand, as soon as religion has closed up "the soul's east window of divine surprise," and is turned into a mechanism of habit, custom, and system, it is killed. Religion thus grown formal and mechanical, though it may still have a disciplinary function in society, is no longer religion in the primary sense. The spring of joy which characterizes true religion has disappeared, the heightening, propulsive tone has vanished. It may linger on as a vestigial superstition, or a semi-automatic performance, but it is *live* religion only so long as it issues from the centre of personal consciousness and has the throb of personal experience in it.

The creative periods in religious progress have come when the crust of custom, the mechanism of habit, has been broken up by the impact of persons who were capable of fresh and original experiences, persons who have shifted the line of march and brought new energies into play, because they have gained new visions and new insights. The Church, it is true, has never in any period quite sunk to the level of tradition and the automatism of habit, for it has always had beneath its system of organization and dogma a current, more or less hidden and subterranean, of vital, inward, spiritual religion, dependent for its power of conviction, not on books, councils, hierarchies or creeds,—not upon anything kept in cold storage,—but on the soul's experiences of eternal Realities. But the main weakness of organized Christianity has been the tendency to settle into a "sacred" form and system.

Our generation has grown weary of ancient traditions and accumulated systems. We have discovered new worlds in all directions by following the sure path of experience, and we can never again settle down with a naive and childlike trust in the house which the past has builded. Our first question in any field is, not What do the scribes and schoolmen say? not What is the unbroken tradition? but, What are the facts? What data does experience furnish? This shifting of centre from "authority" to "experience" runs through all the pursuits of the human spirit in the modern world, and, as would be expected, religion has been profoundly affected by it. In religion as in other fields of inquiry, the questions of moment have come to be those which deal with life. We take slender interest in dogmatic constructions; we turn from these with impatience, and ask for the testimony of the soul, for the basis of religion in the nature of man as man. This profound tendency of the modern world has brought strongly into prominence a mystical type of religion, that is to say, a type of religion which is primarily grounded in experience,[1] and with the tendency has come a corresponding interest in the mystics of the past.

Mysticism is a word which cannot properly be used without careful definition. To many readers it carries no clear and concrete meaning; to others it has an ominous significance and a forbidding sound, as though the safe and beaten track, which the defenders of the faith have builded, were being left for will-o'-the-wisps and wandering lights. I shall use the word mysticism to express the *type of religion which puts the emphasis on immediate awareness of relation with God, on direct and intimate consciousness of the Divine Presence. It is religion in its most acute, intense, and living stage.*

Religion of this mystical type is not confined to Christianity, but belongs, in some degree, to all forms of religion, for first-hand experiences of a Divine and Higher Presence are as old as human personality. Dr. Brinton is undoubtedly right in his contention that "all religions depend for their origin and continuance directly upon inspiration," that is to say, upon direct intercourse.[2] The men who have made religion a living power for any people are, as he says, "persons who have been face to face with God, who have heard His voice and felt His presence."[3] Dr. Tylor has expressed much the same view in his account of the origin of religious experience in the primitive revealers.

"There are times," he says, "when powers and impressions out of the course of the mind's normal action and words that seem spoken by a voice from without, messages of mysterious knowledge, of counsel or warning, seem to indicate the intervention, as it were, of a second, superior soul."[4]

This quotation from Dr. Tylor puts the emphasis on an experience "out of the course of the mind's normal action," and raises the question whether mysticism is something normal or abnormal. Both positions have been strongly defended.

Canon R. C. Moberly says that "Christian mysticism is the doctrine, or rather the experience, of the Holy Spirit—the realization of human personality as characterized by and consummated in the indwelling reality of the Spirit of Christ,

which is God." "It is Christ," he says, "who is the true
mystic; or if the mode of expression be preferred, it is He who
alone has realized all that mysticism and mystics have aimed
at—with more, or with less, whether of disproportion or of
success. And in Him that perfect realization evidently means
a harmony, a sanity, a fitly proportioned completeness. It is
an inward light which makes itself manifest as character; a
direct communion of love which is also, to the fullest extent,
wholly rational at once and wholly practical; it is as much
knowledge as love, and love as knowledge; it is as truly contemplation as activity, and activity as contemplation. In being the ideal of mysticism, it is also the ideal of general, and
of practical, and of *all*, Christian experience. For the most
practical type of Christian experience misconceives itself, until
it conceives itself as an expression, in action, of a central truth,
—that truth of transcendent fact, which practical Christians
are too often content to call 'mystical,' and, so calling it, to
banish, or to try to banish, from the region of practical life."[5]

In Canon Moberly's conception, mysticism is not a special,
exceptional experience, but, rather, a life consummated in the
practice of the Presence of God. It is life in its wholeness as
over against a partial life, which is shut up to some *narrow
compartment* of its true being. This meaning of mysticism is
well brought out by President Henry Churchill King. He says:
"The truly mystical may be summed up as simply a protest in
favour of the whole man—the entire personality. It says that
men can experience, and live, and feel, and do much more
than they can formulate, define, explain, or even fully express.
Living is more than thinking."[6]

Against this account of mysticism can be put a great array
of testimony to show that it is an abnormal condition—a
form of disease, a manifestation of hysteria.[7] The reason for
this difference of view is easy to find. The two sets of writers
are talking about two different things, though under the same
name. For one group the *real* mystic is a person who, by conformity to the goal of life revealed in Christ, has realized his
life upward in full union with God—a way of living which

is as normal as healthy breathing. For the other group, the *real* mystic is a person who exhibits a special form of psychical dissociation. He is "obsessed" with the idea that he is one with God, or he experiences a trance state, a state of "second personality," in which he loses the boundaries of his "primary self," or at least is subject to "incursions" from beyond the threshold of normal consciousness. Such experiences, we must admit, are not *normal*.

There is no question that there are "mystical experiences," *i.e.* experiences in which the subject feels the Divine Presence and has an assurance of union with God, which are abnormal and pathological, but there is no more reason for narrowing the word "mysticism" to cover this type alone than there is for using the word "love" for pathological love alone. Every form of human experience is capable of an exaggerated, an abnormal state, and there is always a shadowy borderland where it is extremely difficult to draw the line between the normal and the abnormal. This is peculiarly true of religious experience, and mystical experience may stretch over all the degrees from the most perfect sanity to utter disorganization of the self.

I shall first consider mysticism in its normal aspect, as a type of religion which is characterized by an immediate consciousness of personal relationship with the Divine. Something of this sort is familiar to the sanest and most matter-of-fact person among us. There is a mystical aspect in our highest moral moments. We never rise to any high level of moral action without feeling that the "call" of duty comes from beyond our isolated self. There is an augustness in conscience which has made men in all ages name it the voice of God; but however it is named, everybody in these high moments of obedience has an experience which is essentially mystical—an experience which cannot be analysed and reduced to "explanation" in terms of anything else. The great ethical writers of all schools recognize this. "What is good," says Paulsen, "will in the last analysis be decided by immediate incontrovertible *feeling, in which the innermost essence of*

the being [*i.e.* the personality] *manifests itself.* It is as impossible
to force a man by logical proofs to love and admire an ideal of
life as it is to make his tongue feel the sweetness or bitterness
of a particular fruit."[8] "The idea of the Good," says Hastings
Rashdall, "is something simple, ultimate, and unanalysable."
"Moral obligation is one of those immediate data of consciousness from which the idea of God may be inferred."[9]
Professor Sidgwick says that, "Right and wrong as peculiar
to moral cognition are unique and unanalysable."[10] "Duty,"
says Martineau, "involves the discovery of something higher
than ourselves that has claims upon us."[11]

There is likewise a mystical element in prayer whenever it
rises to the level of real communion, or, as Lowell puts it,
when, "stirred below the conscious self," the soul feels

That perfect disenthralment which is God.[12]

Everybody who prays knows the difference between saying
words and phrases, uttering requests, proffering petitions, and
coming into vital communion with God. There are moments of
prayer when the soul feels itself face to face with ultimate
Reality and in joyous fellowship with perfect Personality.
This latter experience is as normal as the lower form of prayer
is, but they are worlds apart in significance and value. It is
because prayer does rise to the height of actual fellowship
with a Divine Companion that men who accept the conclusions
of modern science go on praying, undisturbed by the reign of
law. They are not concerned about the superficial question,
whether prayers are answered or not; for prayer is its own
reward, is an end in itself and carries the person who truly
prays into a joyous state which transcends explanation. As
S. T. Coleridge has well expressed it:—

A sense o'er all my soul impressed
That I am weak, yet not unblessed,
Since in me, round me, everywhere,
Eternal strength and wisdom are.

These mystical experiences in a perfectly sane and normal

fashion often come over whole groups of persons in times of worship. There are times when, in the hush and silence, with no appeal to the senses, and with nothing outward to stir emotion, low breathings of a diviner life are clearly felt and the entire group is fused and baptized into one spirit. There comes the experience of a great refreshing, a release of energy, as though a hidden circuit had been closed.

> For a moment on the soul
> Falls the rest that maketh whole,
> Falls the endless peace.[13]

These are the times when the soul feels its real powers and when the possibilities of life are discovered, and they make the ordinary performances of religious service seem, in comparison, poor and dry. Such experiences are beyond explanation, but they are not abnormal.

There is, too, a mystical element of this normal type in any genuine *faith*. I am not speaking, of course, of a faith which consists in believing something on authority, for that is faith of a lower order. Faith in the primary sense is a way of corresponding with Realities which transcend sense-experience. It is an inward power by which the soul lives above the seen and temporal, and "overcomes" the world of the causal, mechanical order. It is a conviction, arising apparently from the very rationality of the spirit in us, that there is an inner, unseen, spiritual universe—an eternal moral order. It is the soul's vision of *what ought to be* and its confidence in the reality and permanence of that estimate of worth—"the assurance of things hoped for and the evidence of things not seen." It is no mere product of sense-experience, but it is the very pinnacle of rationality and as normal a function as our responses to ocular vision.[14]

It is not an uncommon thing for persons who are entirely free from abnormality to have an experience in which the meaning, the significance, the worth, the richness of life, vastly transcends their concepts and descriptions—when life vastly overflows all that can be said about it. This experience is marked by the emergence of a sort of undifferentiated consciousness like that well known to us when we rise to a high appreciation of the beautiful in nature or art or music. At the highest moments of appreciation there comes, not a loss of consciousness, but the emergence of a new level of consciousness in which neither the *I* nor the *object* is focused in perception or thought.[15] There is in these experiences an absence of self-consciousness, and an absence, too, of the consciousness of any concrete, finite object contemplated, a penetration into a region more real and all-inclusive than that of finite "things."[16]

The poet Coleridge has in many passages called attention to a type of experience which is neither "feeling" nor "knowledge," but something much richer than either alone—an experience which he declares is "the very groundwork" of knowledge, and which arises "when we possess ourselves as one with the whole"—

"An experience deeper than science, more certain than demonstration, and from which flows the sap that circulates through every branch and spray of demonstration and knowledge, an experience which passeth all understanding."[17]

It is now a commonplace of psychology that what we *are* and what we experience vastly transcends our "knowledge" about it; reality overflows at every point our categories of description. Our full self, our *real* self, radiates out from a central pulse of consciousness, which is in the focus of attention, and the part of the self that gets focalized and reduced to conceptual knowledge is only a very tiny fragment. As Maeterlinck has declared: "There is in us, above the reasoning portion of our reason, a whole region answering to something different, which is preparing for the surprises of the future, and which goes on ahead of our imperfect attainments, and enables us to live on a level very much superior to that of those attainments."[18]

Now there are times when this underlying total whole of consciousness comes into power in us in unusual fashion, when the stored-up gains of a lifetime are at our command,

and we seem to possess ourselves even down to the roots of our being. In truth, at times, we are aware of a More than "ourselves" impinging on the skirts of our being. There is no time in our lives, of course, when we do not draw upon this wider consciousness which is the matrix in which our "ideas" and concepts are born. We are all aware how often we arrive at conclusions and actions without reasoning or thinking; how often we deal wisely with situations, without being able to trace the source of our wisdom. The supreme issues of life are settled for us, all the way up and down the scale, by unreasoned adjustments, by intents rather than contents of consciousness, by value-responses, which far overflow any knowledge explanation which we can give. It may, I think, be said that all great work, all work which has the touch of genius on it, comes from persons who in special degrees draw upon this matrix consciousness. Such persons feel often as though a Power not themselves were working through them; as though, without tension or effort, the creation at which they are working was "given" to them or "brought" to them. There are, I repeat, times when in extraordinary ways the dualistic character of ordinary thought is transcended and the soul comes into possession of itself as a whole, when all we have been, or are, or hope to be, becomes real; and not only so, but in these deeper reaches of experience some higher Power than ourselves *seems* to work with us and through us—a larger life, continuous with ourselves, seems to environ us. Our own consciousness appears to be only an effective centre in a vast spiritual environment which acts along with us. As Matthew Arnold has finely said:

A bolt is shot back somewhere in our breast
And a lost pulse of feeling stirs again.

.   .   .   .   .

And then he thinks he knows
The hills where his life rose
And the sea where it goes.[19]

There are persons seemingly as normal as the sanest tiller

of the soil, who find themselves fused into union with a
wider, diviner life than that of their common, everyday experiences, who have times when their soul takes holiday from
doubt and strain and perplexity. A great refreshing floods
them, they are aware of a heightened energy, as though they
had pushed out into a new compartment of being. It is like
the aesthetic experience, in its lofty levels, only the impulse
comes from within instead of from without. There could be no
better account of this heightened life than Edward Dowden
has given in his Sonnet on *Awakening*.

> Suddenly, we know not how, a sound
> Of living streams, an odour, a flower crowned
> With dew, a lark upspringing from the sod,
> And we awake. O joy and deep amaze,
> Beneath the everlasting hills we stand,
> We hear the voices of the morning seas,
> And earnest prophesyings in the land,
> While from the open heaven leans forth at gaze
> The encompassing great cloud of witnesses.

Such lofty aesthetic joy is perhaps unusual, though some
degree of it has probably at some time swept the lives of the
most prosaic of us, and so, too, these floods of religious refreshing from within, these mystical experiences, these times
when we seem to possess the whole of ourselves, may be unusual, but they are not abnormal experiences, nor are they
foreign to our true nature as men.

I have spoken of various types of experience which are in
some degree mystical, and which yet are well within the line
of normal healthy life. There are other types of mystical experience which may, and often do, pass over the border-line
of normality and occasionally, at least, exhibit pathological
phenomena. Among all peoples that have left any annals there
have been persons of extraordinary powers: soothsayers, magi-
cians, wizards, witches, medicine-men, sibyls, clairvoyants,
seers, prophets, persons "possessed" by superhuman spirits.
Such persons, sometimes called "divine," and sometimes

called "demoniac," have played an enormous rôle in human history. Dr. Pierre Janet has well expressed the part such men and women have played: "In the development of every great religion, both in ancient and in modern times, there have always been strange persons who raised the admiration of the crowd because their nature seemed to be different from human nature. Their manner of thinking was not the same as that of the others; they had extraordinary oblivions or remembrances, they had visions, they saw or heard what others could not see or hear. They were illumined by odd convictions; not only did they think but they also felt in another way than the bulk of mankind; they had an extraordinary delicacy of certain senses joined to extravagant insensibilities, which enabled them to bear the most dreadful tortures with indifference or even with delight. Not only did they feel, but they also lived otherwise than other people; they could do without sleep, or sleep for months together; they lived without eating or drinking, without satisfying their natural needs. Is it not such persons who have always excited the religious admiration of peoples, whether sibyls, prophets, pythonesses of Delphi or Ephesus, or saints of the Middle Ages, or ecstatics, or illuminates? Now they were considered as worthy of admiration and beatified, now they were called witches or demoniacs and burnt; but, at the bottom, they always caused astonishment, and they played a great part in the development of dogmas and creeds."[20]

The literature of mysticism abounds with cases of ecstasy, of vision of "light," audition of "voices," and there are well-authenticated instances of automatisms and even of "stigmata." Again and again there have come to men and women sudden "incursions" or "invasions" from beyond the margin of personal consciousness, and these persons have *felt* themselves environed with God or even united in one life with Him.[21] Are these unusual and more or less abnormal experiences instances of pathology, cases of hysteria, or are they evidences of Divine Influence and Divine Presence? The mystic himself believes that he has an *experience of God* because (1) these experiences of his come from beyond the margin of his individual *me;* (2) there is something in the content of his experience which transcends anything that normally belongs to him in his finiteness; and (3) these experiences possess an impelling, coercive power, a higher unification of life than he ordinarily knows.[22]

But does this sort of subjective experience furnish empirical evidence of God? May not what, in his own personal vision, the mystic calls "an experience of God" be only the result of an unconscious "suggestion" and no more a proof of God than everyday, common experience is? Recent studies of hysteria and hypnotism have revolutionized all our ideas of the psychological range and scope and the subtle power of suggestion.[23] Society abounds with persons who are hypersensitive to suggestion and over-acute to imitate attitudes and experiences which occur within their environment, or are suggested by their reading, and there is no lack of persons who are swayed by impulses which seem to rise mysteriously within themselves by unconscious *auto-suggestion.*

Some aspects of the experience of mystics undoubtedly are due to suggestion. There have been mystics who have possessed abnormal constitutions, who were subject to strange psychical disturbances. It is certain that many of the abnormal phenomena reported in the lives of mystics are in no way distinguishable from similar phenomena in hysterical cases. Trances, losses of consciousness, automatisms, vision of lights, audition of voices, "stigmata," and such-like experiences, are evidences of hysteria, and they are not in themselves evidences of Divine Influence or of Divine Presence. In fact, many mystics have practised methods of asceticism which were adapted to turn them into abnormal persons and to produce in them hysterical constitutions. They have "worked themselves up" to abnormal states. In the light of these facts it has been contended that even those striking experiences of expansion, enlargement, absorption in the Infinite, freedom from all limits, ecstatic joy, which mystics exhibit, may be instances of auto-suggestion.[24] It is quite possible to be so absorbed in a single thought that all consciousness of body sensations, all awareness of an external world, all things of time and space, shall be unnoticed and be as though they were not, and when all strain and muscular tension are absent, peace and joy and fulness of life are the natural result. It is easy to produce such a state through hypnotic suggestion, and it seems plainly within the range of auto-suggestion.

We cannot, therefore, with implicit confidence, leap to the conclusion that every instance of so-called mystical experience furnishes us with a sure clue to the God Whom our eager souls seek. To the mystic himself the experience is evidence enough. It lights his lamp and girds his loins for action; it floods him with new power; it banishes doubt and despair as the sunrise banishes darkness. He no more wants arguments now to prove God's existence than the artist wants arguments to prove the reality of beauty or the lover does to prove the worth of love.

But it is useless to claim that mystical experiences have such ontological bearing that they settle for *everybody* the reality of God. No subjective experience, however momentous and significant it may be for the person who has it, can settle for everybody else the question: Is there in the universe a God who is personal and all-loving? No empirical experience of any sort can ever answer that question, and to the end of the world men will be called upon to walk by *faith*, to make their venture in the light of what ought to be true, and in the light of what seems to them true, and to live by that faith.

But while these inward mystical experiences cannot be pushed to the extreme of being turned into compelling ontological proofs, they nevertheless do offer a very weighty ground for believing that there is a More of Consciousness continuous with our own—a co-consciousness with which our own is bound up, and that constructive influences do come into us from beyond ourselves.[25] We must not take fright at the word *auto-suggestion*. It is only a word, a phrase, which explains nothing. We have not eliminated God when we conclude, as we must do, that the physical universe has evolved.

"Evolution" is only a fresh word for describing the method of making a universe. And when we have named these great spiritual crises, which carry men up to new levels of life and power and service, "auto-suggestive experiences," we have only substituted one word for another. We called them "new births"; we call them "auto-suggestions"! The *fact* remains on our hands, and the fact is a momentous one.

There have been religious geniuses in all ages and in all countries, who have had experiences of spiritual expansion. They have been made aware of a Realm of Reality on a higher level than that revealed through their senses. They have sometimes felt invaded by the inrush of larger Life; sometimes they have seemed to push a door inward into a larger range of being, with vastly heightened energy. The experience is, as we have seen, always one of joy and rapture; in fact, it is probably the highest joy a mortal ever feels. But the significant fact is not the sense of expansion, or of freedom, or of joy. It is not something merely subjective. It is that such experiences minister to life, construct personality and conduce to the increased power of the race—*energy to live by actually does come to them from somewhere*. The universe backs the experience.

We cannot lightly pass over the spiritual service of mystics. Far from being the unpractical, dreamy persons they are too often conceived to have been, they have weathered storms, endured conflicts, and lived through water-spouts which would have overwhelmed souls whose anchor did not reach beyond the veil. They have discovered an inner refuge, where they enjoy the truce of God, even amid the din of the world's warfare. They have led great reforms, championed movements of great moment to humanity, and they have saved Christianity from being submerged under scholastic formalism and ecclesiastical systems, which were alien to man's essential nature and need. They have been spiritual leaders, they are the persons who shifted the levels of life for the race.[26] They have been able to render these services because they felt themselves allied inwardly with a larger personal Power than themselves, and they have been aware that they were in immediate correspondence with Some One—a Holy Spirit, a Great Companion—who was working with them and through them. This *furtherance of life* by incoming energy, the heightening of power by correspondence with what *seems* to be God, is, however, by no means confined to a few chosen spirits and rare geniuses; it is a widespread fact to be reckoned with everywhere. There are multitudes of men and women in out-of-the-way places, in backwoods towns, and on uneventful farms, who are the salt of the earth and the light of the world in their communities, because they have had experiences which revealed to them Realities which their neighbours missed, and powers to live by which the mere "church-goers" failed to find.

We have thus much more to account for and explain than a few rare, subjective experiences, a few cases of heightened *feeling*. We are bound to realize that mystic experiences have a life-value, and validate themselves in action. Those who are finely sensitive to wider spheres of Reality impinging on their inner realm, and who correspond and co-operate with that More which seems continuous and conterminous with their lives, gain not only in *capacity* to correspond and co-operate, but also in power to overcome difficulties, and to put their lives into constructive service. We have on our hands experiences which have opened to individuals and to the race as a whole wider realms of being, experiences which have heightened the quality of life and which have given new energy of survival, and we are compelled to conclude, either that the personal self is a bottomless affair, carrying within itself infinite unexplored chambers and undreamed-of energies which sometimes come into play, or that the personal self is bosomed on a larger Realm of Consciousness from which we draw our being into the bounds of individuality, and with which we may *correspond*. It has been, as we shall see, the contention of mystics in all ages that God Himself is the ground of the soul, and that in the deeps of their being all men partake of one central Divine Life. The facts, at any rate, all point in this direction.

It is true that the great mystics have often possessed peculiar psychical constitutions. They have sometimes exhibited the phenomena of hysteria, and sometimes they have, beyond question, been pathological, and have experienced abnormal states due to an unstable nervous system. But it is also true that persons possessing such psychical constitutions have in unusual ways, and in heightened degree, been able to correspond with an environing Reality which built up and vitalised their personal lives. Again and again this "correspondence" has brought them health and a unified and ordered will. They *seem* to find themselves enveloped in a matrix-consciousness of far wider reach than that of which ordinary persons are conscious, and they demonstrate that their "correspondence" has life-value and a value for the race.

There is thus some co-relation between these inward experiences and the Eternal Nature of Things. They have functioned to the enlargement of personal life and to the expansion of human society. It is just these persons who have had first-hand experiences of dealing with inward Reality, that *seems* to be God, who have been the master builders of religion. Their testimony to unseen Realities gives the clue and stimulus to multitudes of others to gain a like experience, and it is, too, their testimony that makes God real to the great mass of men who are satisfied to believe on the strength of another's belief. They have, stage by stage, advanced the realm of spiritual life and the appreciation of it, just as great musicians have enlarged the realm of sound-harmonies and the appreciation of them.

It is no discredit to inward, mystical religion to show that social suggestion, or even auto-suggestion, has played a great part in the development of it. Both have played a great part in the development of all experiences. Our language, our moral ideals, our human fashions, are all what they are because of the conscious or unconscious influence of group-suggestion, for our lives are, to a greater extent than most persons realize, conjunct with our fellows. And "auto-suggestion" may be only another way of saying that God and man are conjunct, and that in the deeps of the soul, beyond our power of knowing how, Divine suggestions come to human consciousness. The fact is, that enlarging, expanding power, constructive spiritual energy, comes into certain persons, which makes them sure that they are allied to a Being who guarantees the ultimate goodness of the world. They hear

> The bubbling of the springs
> That feed the world,

and they live more dynamic lives because of these experiences which rise within them

> as mysteriously as cape
> Of cloud grown out of invisible air.

But this experience, as soon as it is valued and appreciated, will, let us grant, show the influence of unconscious suggestion from the social environment, and will be found to have a temporal element in it. The actual mystical *views* of any given period, the symbolism through which these inward experiences are expressed, the "revelations" which come to mystical prophets, all bear the mark and colour of their particular age. There are no "pure experiences," *i.e.* no experiences which come wholly from *beyond* the person who has them.

The most refined mysticism, the most exalted spiritual experience is *partly* a product of the social and intellectual environment in which the personal life of the mystic has formed and matured. There are no experiences of any sort which are independent of preformed expectations or unaffected by the prevailing beliefs of the time. Every bit of our inner or outer life, however much it is our own, is shot through with lines of colour due to social and racial suggestions. All our ideals of goodness, all our instantaneous decisions of conscience, our most inward light, and our most instinctive wisdom, have come to be what they are because we have been organic with our particular social group at this identical period of human

history. Mystical experiences will be, perforce, saturated with
the dominant ideas of the group to which the mystic belongs,
and they will reflect the expectations of that group and that
period.[27]

It is this conformation of mysticism to the type of religion
out of which it springs, and the fact that it is always imbedded
in the life of a social group that gives it its sanity and safe-
guard from vagaries and caprices. The greatest danger from
mysticism, and there are dangers, is just *this* of becoming
relatively detached from the experience of the race, the illumination of the great revealers of the past. Religion and
morality are the consummate gains of the travail of the ages,
and no person can cut loose from the spiritual group-life in
which he is rooted without entailing serious loss. To sever
one's roots in history and in the slowly-gathered content of
religious faith, "to build all inward" and to have no light
but what comes "pure" by the inward way, is to suffer
shrinkage, and to run the tremendous risk of ending in moral
and spiritual bankruptcy, with only vagaries and caprices for
assets. The sane mystic does not exalt his own experiences
over historical revelation, he rather interprets his own openings in the light of the master-revelations. He does not fool-
ishly conclude, because he has a vision of his own, that "the
glory of God in the face of Jesus Christ" is out-dated and
unnecessary, any more than the artist, with a "gift" of his
own, concludes that he has no need of the inspiring guidance
of the old masters; or than the musician, who has an original
creative power in himself, flies to the conclusion that he can
ignore the men in the past who have revealed the nature and
scope of music. Mystical religion, instead of making the soul
independent of Christ and of earlier revelations, rather insists
that every hint of the Divine meaning that has come in any
age, through any person, is precious, and that the supreme
unveiling of the nature and character of God, the highest
exhibition of the range and scope of human possibility in the
person of Jesus Christ, is unspeakably important for any one
whose main concern is to be a son of God. This religion of

first-hand experience is not a substitute for Christianity; it is
Christianity alive and vocal in personal experience and in
individual love.

There has undoubtedly been in many mystical movements
an over-emphasis on ecstasy and moveless contemplation, and
it is easy to see that individual mystics have, perhaps unconsciously, employed methods now familiar to us in hypnotic
experiments. They have used short cuts and unspiritual aids
to hasten their arrival at a state of joyous absorption. They
have exhibited an over-fascination for a suspension of all desire
and a loss of the strain and struggle, which go with that
"slow, dead heave of the will" in the great moral issues of
life. They have, too, sometimes been almost obsessed with the
fixed idea that all the ills of life and the confusions of mutability would disappear if only they believed implicitly enough
in the allness of God and the unity of all that is. This has
led them to glorify abstraction and to choose the *via negativa*,
the negative path; that is, to win their peace by refusing to
take account of multiplicity and evil, sin and pain. They have
found their line of least resistance to be withdrawal and negation, which is, at best, only the backstairs to the Upper Room.

But I prefer to dwell on the tremendous service of the
Mystics. There are imperfections in all human undertakings,
and there are blunderers wherever men seriously gird themselves for high endeavours. We do not scorn poetry, though
there have been poetasters who became popular; we do not
give up our appreciation of great music, though there have
been poor performers who got the large gate receipts. We must
recognise the limitations and the false trails, but we do well
to keep in the goodly fellowship of those who have seen and
heard and handled the Word of Life, and who have found the
inner way home.

There is no attempt in the following chapters to give a
complete history of Christian mysticism, nor are all the movements herein studied properly called mystical, though they
have all helped to further religion of this inward and first-
hand type. There have been momentous epochs when vital,

dynamic religion has *flourished*, when men of creative power have made new discoveries of the soul's capacities, and have become so initiated into the mysteries of the kingdom of God that they could open for their fellows new doors into the spiritual life, and thus have become centres of spiritual groups. I shall study, in the following pages, some of these spiritual groups, these creative movements, and some of the persons who have been in a peculiar degree prophets of the soul by virtue of their own direct experience. It is not always possible to trace a *direct* historical connection between these spiritual groups, for the literary data which have survived are often meagre; but the following chapters will make it evident, I think, that there has been a continuous prophetical procession, a mystical brotherhood through the centuries, of those who have lived by the soul's immediate vision. Again and again, as will appear, the writings of a mystic, long dead and seemingly forgotten, with no school of disciples to disseminate his message, have reached an apt and ready soul, have kindled him to glowing life, and have made him again the centre of a new group; and so the torch has passed on to a new age.

I have begun with a brief study of the inward, free, and untrammelled type of religion which prevailed in the early period of the primitive Church, and I have, in the most compact way possible, sketched the growth and development of the ecclesiastical system which was gradually substituted for the free and organic *fellowship* of the first stage of Christianity. The studies of the mystical element in the Church Fathers and in Greek Philosophy are necessarily inadequate. I have confined myself to the task of gathering up the main lines of influence which reappear in the mystical sects of medieval Europe. I have included in these studies the Waldensian, the Wyclifite, and the Anabaptist movements, though they are mainly unmystical, because of their very great importance in the general movement of Christianity toward a more inward and personal form of religion, less ecclesiastical and sacerdotal, and depending more on the direct relation of man to God.

I propose, at some later time, to publish a volume on Jacob

Boehme, and I have thought it best not to crowd his contribution into an inadequate chapter.[28] My studies come down only to the end of the English Commonwealth, because this volume is intended to be an introduction to a series of historical volumes by myself and others devoted to the development and spiritual environment of a particular branch of modern Christianity—The Society of Friends—a religious body which has made a serious attempt to unite inward, mystical religion with active, social endeavours, and to maintain a religious fellowship without a rigid ecclesiastical system, and with large scope for personal initiative, immediate revelation and individual responsibility.

NOTES

1. "The mystic is a thorough-going empiricist" (Josiah Royce, *The World and the Individual*, vol. i. p. 81).

2. D. G. Brinton's *Religions of Primitive People*, p. 52.

3. *Ibid.* p. 58.

4. Dr. E. B. Tylor, *Primitive Culture*, vol. i. p. 182.

5. Canon R. C. Moberly, *Atonement and Personality*, pp. 312–16.

6. H. C. King's *Theology and Social Consciousness*, p. 77.

7. Murisier, *Les Maladies du sentiment religieux*. P. M. T. Janet, "Une Extatique," in *Bulletin de l'Institut psychologique*, Paris, 1901. J. H. Leuba, "Tendances fondamentales des mystiques chrétiens," in *Revue philosophique*, vol. liv.

8. Fr. Paulsen, *A System of Ethics*, p. 11.

9. Hastings Rashdall, *The Theory of Good and Evil*, vol. ii. pp. 103–106.

10. *Mind*, vol. xxviii. p. 580.

11. James Martineau, *Types of Ethical Theory*, vol. ii. p. 104.

12. J. R. Lowell, *The Cathedral*.

13. F. W. H. Myers' *Sunrise*.

14. The question has been raised whether Mystical-religion is higher or lower than Faith-religion (see article by Dr. Lyman in *American Journal of Theology* for July 1904). It is hardly a fair question to raise, since mysticism at every point involves faith; and any faith which is really alive and dynamic is rooted and grounded in first-hand experience.

15. "The aesthetic object and the consciousness in which it arises are no longer held apart. The self becomes identified with the object as peculiarly its own." (Dr. W. D. Furry's *Aesthetic Experience: Its Nature and Function in Epistemology* (Baltimore, 1908), p. 49.)

16. Wordsworth has described a personal experience in a beautiful passage:
> "Sensation, soul and form
> All melted into him; they swallowed up
> His animal being; in them did he live,
> And by them did he live; they were his life.
> In such access of mind, in such high hours
> Of visitation from the living God,
> Thought was not; in enjoyment it expired.
> No thanks he breathed, he proffered no request;
> Rapt into still communion that transcends
> The imperfect offices of prayer and praise,
> His mind was a thanksgiving to the power
> That made him; it was blessedness and love.

The Excursion, BOOK i.

There is no better first-hand account of such an unanalysable whole of experience than Mozart's description of the *coming* of a symphony into his consciousness.

"When and how my ideas come I know not, nor can I force them. Those that please me I retain in my memory and am accustomed, as I have been told, to hum them to myself. If I continue in this way, it soon occurs to me how I may turn this or that morsel to account. . . . All this fires my soul, and, provided I am not disturbed, my subject enlarges itself, becomes methodized and defined, and the whole, though it be long, stands almost complete and finished in my mind, so that I can survey it like a fine picture, or a beautiful statue at a glance. Nor do I hear in my imagination the parts *successively*, but I hear them as it were all at once. What a delight this is I cannot express. All this inventing, this producing, takes place in a pleasing, lively dream. But the actual hearing of the whole together is after all the best. And this is perhaps the best gift I have my Divine Master to thank for" (Holmes' *Life and Correspondence of Mozart* (London, 1845), pp. 317–18).

17. S. T. Coleridge's *The Friend*, Essay XI.
18. Cited in J. B. Pratt's *Psychology of Belief*, p. 27.
19. Matthew Arnold's *Buried Life*.
20. P. M. T. Janet, *Major Symptoms of Hysteria*, New York, 1907, p. 8.
21. It would be quite easy to make an entire volume of selections of instances. The four instances given below will illustrate the type I am discussing.

Eckhart declares: "I am as certain as that I live that nothing is so near to me as God. God is nearer to me than I am to myself (Meister Eckhart's *Mystische Schriften*, by Gustav Landaur, p. 96).

Jacob Boehme says: "In one quarter of an hour I saw and knew more than if I had been many years in a university. I saw and knew the being of all things, the Byss and Abyss." Jacob Behmen's [Boehme] *Theo. Phil.* by Edward Taylor (London, 1691), p. 425.

Madame Guyon, to whom mystic experiences were almost common occurrences, gives the following description of one of these: "My spirit disenthralled, became united with and lost in God. And this was so much the case that I seemed to see and know God only, and not myself."

NOTES 77

James Russell Lowell's "revelation," as he himself calls it, is a very good instance of this *experience:* "As I was speaking, the whole system (of the universe) rose up before me like a vague destiny looming from the Abyss. I never before so clearly felt the Spirit of God in me and around me. The whole room seemed to me full of God. The air seemed to waver to and fro with the presence of something, I knew not what. I spoke with the calmness and clearness of a prophet" (*Letters of Lowell*, vol. i. p. 75).

22. See Henri Delacroix, *Étude d'histoire et de psychologie du Mysticisme* (Paris, 1908), pp. 365–66. This is one of the most important books on mysticism that has appeared in recent years.

23. The reader should consult P. M. T. Janet's *Major Symptoms of Hysteria*, New York, 1907.

24. I am dwelling at some length on the place of "suggestion" and "auto-suggestion" because it has been assumed by some recent writers, notably by Professor G. A. Coe, that mystical experiences are only cases of "auto-suggestion" (see Professor Coe's article on "Sources of the Mystical Revelation" in the *Hibbert Journal* for January 1908, pp. 359–72.

25. See William James' *Varieties of Religious Experience*, p. 515.

26. Professor Josiah Royce has very well treated the social service of the Mystics in his *World and the Individual*, vol. i. pp. 85–87.

27. This feature of mystical experience is well treated in Delacroix, *op. cit.*

28. Four chapters—pp. 151–234—in my volume, *Spiritual Reformers*, deal with Jacob Boehme, his message and his influence, and he is there fitted into his place in the succession of spiritual reformers.

2

Spiritual Reformers in the 16th and the 17th Centuries

THERE is no magic in words, though, it must be confessed, they often exercise a psychological influence so profound and far-reaching that they seem to possess a miracle-working efficacy. Some persons live all their lives under the suggestive spell of certain words, and it sometimes happens that an entire epoch is more or less dominated by the mysterious fascination of a sacred word, which needs only to be spoken on the house-top to set hearts beating and legs marching.

"Spiritual" has always been one of these wonder-working words. St. Paul, in Christian circles, was the first to give the word its unique value. For him it named a new order of life and a new level of being. In his thought, a deep cleavage runs through the human race and divides it into two sharply-sundered classes, "psychical men" and "pneumatical men"—men who live according to nature, and men who live by the life of the Spirit. The former class, that is psychical men, are of the earth earthy; they are, as we should say to-day, *empirical*, parts of a vast nature-system, doomed, as is the entire system, to constant flux and mutability and eventually to irretrievable wreck and ruin; the natural, psychical, corruptible man cannot inherit incorruption.[1] On the other hand, the pneumatical or spiritual man "puts on" incorruption and immortality. He is a member of a new order; he is "heavenly," a creation "not made with hands," but wrought out of the substance of the spiritual world, and furnished with the inherent capacity of eternal duration, so that "mortality is swallowed up of life."[2]

This word, thus made sacred by St. Paul's great use of it to designate the new race of the saved, was made the bearer in

the Johannine writings of a no less exalted message, which
has become a living and indissoluble part of the religious consciousness of the Christian world. "Eternal life"—or, what
in these writings is the same thing, "life"—comes through
the reception of the Spirit, in a birth from above. "That
which is born of the flesh is flesh, and that which is born of
the Spirit is Spirit."[3] When the Spirit comes as the initiator
of this abundant life, then we "know that we abide in Him
and He in us, because He hath given us of His Spirit," and it
becomes possible for the Spirit-led person to be guided "into
all the truth," to "love even as He loved," and to "overcome the world."[4] Here, again, the human race is divided
into those who have "received of the Spirit," and those who
have not so received; those who are "born from above" and
those who have had only a natural birth; the twice-born and
the once-born; those who are "of the Spirit," i.e. spiritual,
and those who are "of this world," i.e. empirical.

The Gnostic sects of the second century had one common
link and badge; they all proposed a "way," often bizarre and
strange-sounding to modern ears, by which the soul, astray,
lost, encumbered, or imprisoned in matter, might attain its
freedom and become spiritual. Most of the Gnostic teachers,
who in their flourishing time were as thick as thistle-downs
in summer, conceived of man as consisting of two "halves"
which corresponded with two totally different world-orders.
There was in man, or there belonged to man (1) a visible
body, which was again dichotomized, and believed to be
composed, according to many of the Gnostics, of a subtle
element like that of which they supposed Adam in his un-
fallen state was made, which they named the hylic body, and
a sheath of gross earthy matter which they called the choical
body.[5] There was also (2) another, invisible, "half," generally divided into lower and higher stories. The lower story,
the psychical, was created or furnished by the Demiurge, or
sub-divine creator of the natural system, while the top-story,
or pneumatical self, was a spiritual seed derived from the supreme spiritual Origin, the Divine Pleroma, the Fulness of

the Godhead. Those who possessed this spiritual seed were "the elect," "the saved," who eventually, stripped of their sheath of matter and their psychical dwelling, would be able to pass all "the keepers of the way," and rise to the pure spiritual life.

The Montanists launched in the second century a movement, borne along on a mountain-wave of enthusiasm, for a "spiritual" Church composed only of "spiritual" persons. They called themselves "the Spirituals," and they insisted that the age or dispensation of the Spirit had now come. The Church, rigidly organized with its ordained officials, its external machinery, and its accumulated traditions, was to them part of an old and outworn system to be left behind. In the place of it was to come a new order of "spiritual people" of whom the Montanist prophets were the "first fruits,"—a new and peculiar people, born from above, recipients of a divine energizing power, partakers in the life of the Spirit and capable of being guided on by progressive revelations into all the truth. To be "spiritual" in their vocabulary meant to be a participator in the Life of God, and to be a living member of a group that was led and guided by a continuously self-revealing Spirit. This Spirit was conceived, however, not as immanent and resident, not as the indwelling and permeative Life of the human spirit, but as foreign and remote, and He was thought of as "coming" in sporadic visitations to whom He would, His coming being indicated in extraordinary and charismatic manifestations.

This type of "spiritual religion," though eventually stamped out in the particular form of Montanism, reappeared again and again, with peculiar local and temporal variations, in the history of Christianity.[6] To the bearers of it, the historic Church, with its crystallized system and its vast machinery, always seemed "unspiritual" and traditional. They believed, each time the movement appeared, that *they* had found the way to more abundant life, that the Spirit had come upon them in a special manner, and was through them inaugurating a higher order of Christianity, and they always felt that their religion of direct experience, of invading energy, of inspirational insights, of charismatic bestowals, and of profound emotional fervour was distinctly "spiritual," as contrasted with the historic Church which claimed indeed a divine origin and divine "deposits," but which, as they believed, lacked the continuous and progressive leadership of the Spirit. They were always very certain that their religion was characteristically "spiritual," and all other forms seemed to them cold, formal, or dead. In their estimates, men were still divided into spiritual persons and psychical persons—those who lived by the "heart" and those who lived by the "head."

Parallel with the main current of the Protestant Reformation, a new type of "spiritual religion" appeared and continued to manifest itself with mutations and developments, throughout the entire Reformation era, with a wealth of results which are still operative in the life of the modern world. The period of this new birth was a time of profound transition and ferment, and a bewildering variety of roads was tried to spiritual Canaans and new Jerusalems, then fondly believed to be near at hand. It is a long-standing tragedy of history that the right wing of a revolutionary or transforming movement must always suffer for the unwisdom and lack of balance of those who constitute the left, or extreme radical, wing of the movement. So it happened here. The nobler leaders and the saner spirits were taken in the mass with those of an opposite character, and were grouped under comprehensive labels of reproach and scorn, such as "Antinomians," "Enthusiasts," or "Anabaptists," and in consequence still remain largely neglected and forgotten.

The men who initiated and guided this significant undertaking—the exhibition in the world of what they persistently called "spiritual religion"—were influenced by three great historic tendencies, all three of which were harmoniously united in their type of Christianity. They were the Mystical tendency, the Humanistic or Rational tendency, and the distinctive Faith-tendency of the Reformation. These three

strands are indissolubly woven together in this type of so-
called spiritual religion. It was an impressive attempt,
whether completely successful or not, to widen the sphere
and scope of religion, to carry it into *the whole of life*, to ground
it in the very nature of the human spirit, and to demonstrate
that to be a man, possessed of full life and complete health, is
to be religious, to be spiritual. I propose, as a preliminary
preparation for differentiating this special type of "spiritual
religion," to undertake a study, as brief as possible, of these
three underlying and fundamental strands or tendencies in
religion which will, of course, involve some consideration of
the inherent nature of religion itself.

For my present purpose it is not necessary to study the
twilight history of religion in primitive races nor to trace
its origins in the cradle-stage of human life. Anthropologists
are rendering a valuable service in their attempts to explore
the baffling region of primitive man's mind, and they have
hit upon some very suggestive clues, though so far only
tentative ones, to the psychological experiences and attitudes
which set man's feet on the momentous religious trail. At
every stage of its long and devious history, religion has been
*some sort of life-adjustment to realities which were felt to be of su-
preme importance either to the individual or to the race,* and it
becomes thus possible for the scientific observer to note a
developmental process and to discover a principle which links
it in with a universal scheme of evolution.

But religion can never be adequately treated either in terms
of racial origins or of biological history, though there can
be no doubt whatever that there are genetic and biological
factors to be considered. Nor, again, can religion be adequately and exhaustively dealt with by the psychological
method of investigation. The psychological studies of religion
in recent years have greatly enriched our knowledge of the
range and scope and power of man's psychic nature and functions, of his instincts, desires, valuations, needs, yearnings,
beliefs, and modes of activity and behaviour, and particularly
of the important influence which the social group has exer-

cised and still exercises in the furtherance of religious attitudes and ideals. But the psychological method has obvious
and inherent limitations. Like any other natural science,
psychology is limited to description and causal explanation
of the phenomena of its special field, which in this case is
states of consciousness. It does not pretend, or even aspire, to
pronounce upon the ultimate nature of consciousness, nor
upon the moral significance of personality. Psychology is as
empirical as any other science. It modestly confines its scope
of research to what *appears* in finite and describable forms.
It possesses no ladder by which it can transcend the empirical
order, the fact-level. The religion which the psychologist reports upon is necessarily stripped of all transcendental and objective reference. Its wings are severely clipped. It is only one
of man's multitudinous *reactions* in the presence of the facts
of his time and space world. It is nakedly subjective and
works, not because there is Something or Some One beyond,
which answers it, and corresponds with its up-reach, but only
because undivided faith-attitudes always liberate within the
field of consciousness energy for life-activity.

We need not blame the psychologist for this radical reduction of the age-long pretensions of religion. If he is to bring
religion over into the purview of the scientific field, he can
do nothing else but reduce it. Science can admit into its world
nothing that successfully defies descriptive treatment. The
poet may know of flowers which "can give thoughts that do
often lie too deep for tears," but science discovers no such
flowers in its field. Its flowers are amazingly complex, but they
call for no handkerchief. They are merely aggregations of
describable parts, each of which has well-defined functions.
The "man" whom science studies is complicated almost beyond belief. He is an aggregation of trillions of cells. He is
such a centre of vibrations that a cyclone is almost a calm
compared to the constant cyclic storms within the area of
man's corporeal system. His "mental states" have their en-
tries and exits before "the foot-lights of consciousness" and
exhibit a drama more intricate than any which human genius

has conceived. But each "state" is a definite, more or less describable, *fact* or *phenomenon*. For science, "man's" inner life, as well as his corporeal bulk, is an aggregate of empirical items. No loophole is left for freedom—that is for any novel undetermined event. No shekinah remains within for a mysterious "conscience" to inject into this fact-world insights drawn from a higher world of noumenal, or absolute, reality. "Man" is merely a part of the naturalistic order, and has no way of getting out of the vast net in which science catches and holds "all that is."

There is, I repeat, no ground for blaming the psychologist for making these reductions. His science can deal only with an order of facts which will conform to the scientific method, for wherever science invades a field, it ignores or eliminates every aspect of novelty or mystery or wonder, every aspect of reality which cannot be brought under scientific categories, *i.e.* every aspect which cannot be treated quantitatively and causally and arranged in a congeries of interrelated facts occurring according to natural laws. The only cogent criticism is that any psychologist should suppose that his scientific account is the "last word" to be spoken, that his reports contain all the returns that can be expected, or that this method is the only way of approach to truth and reality. Such claims to the rights of eminent domain and such dogmatic assertions of exclusive finality always reveal the blind spot in the scientist's vision. He sees steadily but he does not see wholes. He is of necessity dealing with a reduced and simplified "nature" which he constantly tends to substitute for the vastly richer whole of reality that boils over and inundates the fragment which submits to his categories. We do well to gather in every available fact which biology or anthropology or psychology can give us that throws light on human behaviour, or on primitive cults, or on the richer subjective and social religious functions of full-grown men. But the interior insight got from religion itself, the rich wholeness of religious experience, the discovery within us of an inner nature which defies description and baffles all plumb-

lines, and which *can draw out of itself more than it contains*,
indicate that we here have dealings with a type of reality
which demands for adequate treatment other methods of comprehension than those available to science.

In the old Norse stories, Thor tried to empty the famous
drinking-horn in the games of Utgard, but to his surprise he
found that, though the horn looked small, he could not
empty it, for it turned out that the horn was immersed in the
limitless and bottomless ocean. Again he tried to lift a small
and insignificant-looking animal, but, labour as he might, he
could not lift it, for it was grown into, and was organic with,
the whole world, and could not be raised without raising the
very ground on which the lifter stood! Somewhat so, the
reality of religion is so completely bound up with the whole
personal life of man and with his conjunct life in the social
group and in the world of nature; it is, in short, so much an
affair of man's whole of experience, of his spirit in its undivided and synthetic aspects, that it can never be adequately
dealt with by the analytic and descriptive method of this
wonderful new god of science, however big with results that
method may be.

The interior insight, the appreciation of religion, the rich
and concrete whole of religious consciousness, is, and will
always remain, the primary way to the *secret* of religion—
religion in its "first intention"—as the experience of time-
duration is the only possible way to the elemental meaning
of time. It has in recent years in many quarters become the
fashion to call this "interior insight," this appreciation of
religion from within, "mysticism"; and to assume that here
in mysticism we come upon the very essence of religion. This
conclusion, however, is as narrow and as unwarranted as is
the truncation of religion at the hands of science. The mystical
element in religion is only one element in a vastly richer complex, and it must not be given undue emphasis and imperial
sway in the appreciation of the complete whole of "spiritual
religion." We must, too, carefully discriminate *mystical experience* from the elaborate body of doctrines and theories, his-

torically known as "mysticism," which is as much an *ism* as
are the other typical, partial, and more or less abstract formulations of religion.

Mysticism for the mystic himself is characterized by a personal experience through which the ordinary limitations of
life and the passionate pursuits of the soul are transcended,
and a self-evident conviction is attained that he is in communion, or even in union, with some self-transcending Reality
that absolutely satisfies and is what he has always sought.
"This is He, this is He," the mystic exclaims: "There is no
other: This is He whom I have waited for and sought after
from my childhood !"[7]

The experience is further characterized by the inrush of new
energies as though a mysterious door had been pushed open
—either out or in—admitting the human spirit to wider
sources of life. "Fresh bubblings from the eternal streams of
Life flowing into the soul" is the way the recipient often describes it. All the deep-lying powers of the inward self, usually so divergent and conflicting—the foreground purposes
defeated by background inhibitions, and by doubts on the
border,—become liberated and unified into one conscious life
which is not merely intellectual, nor merely volitional, nor
solely emotional, but an undivided whole of experience, intensely joyous, enriched with insight and pregnant with deeds
of action. As in lofty experiences of appreciation of beauty,
or of music, or when the chords of life are swept by a great
love, or by a momentous moral issue, the spirit rises in mystical experience to a form of consciousness which no longer
marks clock-time and succession of events, whether outward
or inward. It may afterwards take hours or days or weeks or
even years to spread out and review and apprehend and adjust
to the experience—"the opening," to use George Fox's impressive word—but while it is *there* it is held in one unbroken
synthetic time-span. It is, to revive a scholastic phrase, a
totum simul, an all-at-once experience, in which parts, however
many, make one integral whole, as in a melody or in a work
of art; so that the mystic has a real experience of what we try

to express by the word Eternity. It feels as though the usual insulations of our own narrow personal life were suddenly broken through and we were in actual contact with an enfolding presence, life-giving, joy-bringing, and light-supplying.

In instances where the intensity is great, unusual psychological phenomena appear. Sometimes voices are heard, or sounds "like a mighty rushing wind"; sometimes there are automatic visions of light, or of forms or figures, as, for instance, of Christ, or of a cross; sometimes automatic writing or speaking attends the experience; sometimes there are profound body-changes of a temporary, or even permanent character; sometimes there is a state of swoon or ecstacy, lasting from a few seconds to entire days. These physical phenomena, however, are as spiritually unimportant and as devoid of religious significance as are the normal bodily resonances and reverberations which accompany, in milder degrees, all our psychic processes. They indicate no high rank of sainthood and they prove no miracle-working power. The significant features of the experience are the consciousness of fresh springs of life, the release of new energies, the inner integration and unification of personality, the inauguration of a sense of mission, the flooding of the life with hope and gladness, and the conviction, amounting in the mind of the recipient to certainty, that God is found as an environing and vitalizing presence—as the recipient already quoted reports his conviction: "I have met with my God; I have met with my Saviour. I have felt the healings drop upon my soul from under His wings."[8]

If *everybody* had experiences of that sort there would be no more doubt of the existence of an actual spiritual environment in vitalizing contact with the human spirit than there now is of an external world with which we correspond. There is *a priori* no reason against the reality of such an inner spiritual universe. It is precisely as conceivable that constructive and illuminating influences should stream into our inner selves from that central Light with which our inmost self is allied, as that objects in space and time should bombard us with messages adapted to our senses. The difference is that we all experience the outer environment and only a few of us experience the inner. The mystic himself has no doubt—*he sees*, but he cannot give quite his certainty of vision to any one else. He cannot, like "the weird sisters" of Greek story, lend out his eye for others to see with. He can only talk about, or write about, what he has seen, and his words are often words of little meaning to those who lack the vision.

But the very characteristics of mystical religion which give it its self-evidence and power at the same time mark limits to its scope and range. It is and must be primarily and essentially first-hand experience, and yet it is an experience that is by no means universal. It is not, so far as we can see from the facts at hand, an experience which attaches to the very nature of consciousness as such, or indeed one which is bound to occur even when the human subject strains forward all the energies of his will for the adventure, or when by strict obedience to the highest laws of life known to him he *waits* for the high visitation. Some aspect is involved over which the will has no control. Some other factor is implied besides the passion and the purity of the seeking soul. The experience "comes," as an inrush, as an emergence from the deeper levels of the inner life, but the glad recipient does not know how he secured the prize or how to repeat the experience, or how to tell his friend the way to these "master moments" of blessedness.

There are numerous persons who are as serious and earnest and passionate as the loftiest mystical saint, and who, in spite of all their listening for the inner flow of things, discover no inrushes, feel no invasions, are aware of no environing Companion, do not even feel a "More of Consciousness conterminous and continuous with their own." Their inner life appears impervious to divine bubblings. The only visitants that pass over the threshold of their consciousness are their own mental states, now bright and clear, now dim and strange, but all bearing the brand and mark of temporal origin. This type of experience must not, therefore, be insisted on as the only way to God or to the soul's homeland. Spiritual religion must not be put to the hazard of conditions that limit its universality and restrict it to a chosen few. To insist on mystical experience as the only path to religion would involve an "election" no less inscrutable and pitiless than that of the Calvinistic system—an "election" settled for each person by the peculiar psychic structure of his inner self.[9]

There is another limitation which must always attach to religion of the purely mystical type. In so far as it is an *experience* of the inward type, it is indescribable and incommunicable. That does not mean or imply any lessened value in the experience itself, it only means that it is very difficult to mint it into the universal coinage of the world. The recovery of faith, after some catastrophic bankruptcy of spiritual values, as with Job or Dante or Faust, cannot be described in analytic steps. The loss of faith in the rationality of the universe, the collapse of the "beautiful world" within, can be told step by step; the process of integration and reconstruction, on the other hand, always remains somewhat of a mystery, though it is plain enough that a new and richer inner world has been found. So, too, with Mysticism. The experience itself may, and often does, bring to the recipient an indubitable certainty of spiritual realities, revealing themselves within his own spirit, and, furthermore, it is often productive of permanent life-results, such as augmented conviction, heightened tone of joy, increased unification of personality, intense moral passion and larger conquering power, but he, nevertheless, finds it a baffling matter to draw from his mystical experience concrete information about the nature and character of God, or to supply, from the experience alone, definite contributions that can become part of the common spiritual inheritance of the race.

> The soul
> Remembering how she felt, but *what* she felt
> Remembering not, retains an obscure sense
> Of possible sublimity.[10]

There can be, I think, no doubt that the persons whom we call mystics have enormously added to the richness of our conception of God, or that they have made impressive contributions to the capital stock of our religious knowledge. But I question whether these increments of knowledge can be fairly traced to "information" which has entered the world through the secret door of mystical "openings." The conception of God by which we live, and our knowledge of eternal life, are in the main not formed of the material which has mysteriously dropped into the world by means of "sudden incursions," or "oracular communications" through persons of extraordinary psychical disposition. What we get from the mystic, or from the prophet, is not his "experience" but his interpretation, and as soon as he begins to *interpret*, he does so by means of the group-material which the race has gathered in its corporate experience through the ages. The valuable *content* of his message, so far as he succeeds in delivering one, the ideas with which his words are freighted, bear the marks of the slow accumulations of spiritual experience, and they reveal the rich and penetrative influence of the social group in which the mystic's inner life formed and ripened. They have a history as all ideas do.

The real fact of the matter is, that the great mystics are religious geniuses. They make their contribution to religion in ways similar to those in which the geniuses in other fields raise the level of human attainments and achievements. They swiftly seize upon and appreciate the specific achievements of the race behind them; they are profoundly sensitive to the aspirations of their time and to the deep-lying currents of their age; they are suggestible in an acute degree, through heightened interest, to certain ideas or truths or principles which they synthesise by such leaps of insight that slow-footed logic seems to be transcended. Then these unifying and intensifying experiences to which they are subject give them irresistible conviction, "a surge of certainty," a faith of the mountain-moving order, and an increasing dynamic of life which, in the best cases, is manifest in thoughts and words and deeds. Their mystical experience seldom supplies them with a new intellectual content which they communicate, but their experience enables them rather to *see* what they know, to get possession of themselves, and to fuse their truth with the heat of conviction. The mystical experience is thus a way of heightening life and of increasing its dynamic quality rather than a way to new knowledge.

The *negative way*, which has been such a prominent and prevailing characteristic of historical mysticism that many writers have made it the distinct and sufficient differentia of mysticism, has often produced intensity and depth, but it is, nevertheless, a mark of the limitation of this type of religion. The indescribable and undifferentiated character of mystical experience is no doubt partly responsible for the emphatic place which negation has held in mysticism. The experience itself, which seems like "a flight of the alone to the Alone," can be told in no words except those of negation. "The mortal limit of the self" seems loosed, and the soul seems merged into that which it forever seeks but which having found it cannot utter. But the type of metaphysics through which most of the great mystics of history have done their thinking and have made their formulations is still further responsible for the excessive negativity of their systems.

There is, of course, a negative element or aspect in all genuine religion. No person can grow rich in spiritual experience or can gain an intimate acquaintance with a God of purity and truth without negating the easy ways of instinct, the low pursuits of life which end in self, the habits of thought and action which limit and hamper the realization of the diviner possibilities of the whole nature. Sometimes the eye that hinders must be plucked out or the right hand cut off and thrust away for the sake of a freer pursuit of the soul's kingdom. There is, too, a still deeper principle of negativity involved in the very fibre of personal life itself. No one can advance without surrender, no one can have gains without losses, no one can reach great goals without giving up many things in themselves desirable. There is "a rivalry of mes" which no person can ever escape, for in order to choose and achieve one typical self another possible self must be sternly sacrificed. In a very real sense it remains forever true that we must die to live, we must die to the narrow self in order to be raised to the wider and richer self.

But the *negative way* of mysticism is more rigorous and more thorough in its negation than that. Its negations wind up the hill all the way to the very top. Even the *self* must be absolutely negated. "The self, the I, the me and the like, all belong to the evil spirit. The whole matter can be set forth in these words: Be simply and wholly bereft of self." "The I, the me, and the mine, nature, selfhood, the Devil, sin, are all one and the same thing."[11] Not only so, but all *desire* for any particular thing, or any particular experience must be utterly extirpated. "Whatever Good the creature as creature can conceive of and understand is something this or that," and therefore not the One Real Good.[12] "So long as thy soul has an image, it is without simplicity, and so long as it is without simplicity it doth not rightly love God."[13] "Divine love can brook no rival." He who seeks God must "rid himself of all that pertains to the creature." He that would find the absolute Good must withdraw not only beyond all his senses, but beyond all desires, into an inner "solitude where no word is spoken, where is neither creature nor image nor fancy." "Everything depends," Tauler counsels us, "upon a fathomless sinking into a fathomless nothingness. . . . God has really no place to work in but the ground where all has been annihilated. . . . Then when all forms have ceased, in the twinkling of an eye, the man is transformed. . . . Thou must sink into the unknown and unnamed abyss, and above all ways, images, forms, and above all powers, lose thyself, deny thyself, and even unform thyself."[14] The moment the will focusses upon any concrete aim as its goal, it must thereby miss that Good which is above and beyond all particular "things" that can be conceived or named.

But the *negative way* winds up farther still. It ends in the absolutely negative Silent Desert of Godhead "where no one

is at home." Its way up is the way of abstraction and withdrawal from everything finite. He whom the soul seeks cannot
be found in anything "here" or "now"; He must be "yonder."
"It is by no means permitted," says one of the great experts in
negation, "to speak or even to think anything concerning the
super-essential and hidden Deity. . . . It is a Unity above
mind, a One above conception and inconceivable to all conceptions, a Good unutterable by word."[15] "Thou must love
God," Eckhart says, "as not-God, not-Spirit, not-person, not-
image, but as He is, a sheer, pure, absolute One, sundered
from all two-ness and in whom we must eternally sink from
nothingness to nothingness."[16] God, the Godhead, is thus
the absolute "Dark," "the nameless Nothing," an empty
God, a characterless Infinite. "Why dost thou prate of God,"
Eckhart says, "whatever thou sayest of Him is untrue!" The
rapt soul at the end of his road, at the top of the hill, only
knows that every finite account is false and that the only
adequate word is an everlasting Nay.

> Whatever idea your mind comes at,
> I tell you flat
> God is *not* that.[17]

The great mystics have always saved themselves by ne-
glecting to be consistent with this rigorous negation and abstraction. In their practice they have cut through their theory
and gone on living the rich concrete life. But the theory
itself is a false theory of life, and it leads only to a God of
abstraction, not to the God of spiritual religion. The false
trail, however, is to be charged, as I have said, not so much to
mystical experience as to the metaphysics through which the
mystics, not only of Christian communions, but of other
faiths, were compelled to do their thinking. There was no
other way of thinking known to them except this way of
negation. The Infinite was the not-finite; the Absolute was
precisely what the contingent was *not*. The perfect was free
of every mark of imperfection. Behind all manifestations was
the essential Substance which made the manifestations. The

completely Real was above all mutation and process. "For one to assign," therefore, "to God any human attributes," as Spinoza, the supreme apostle of this negative way has said, "is to reveal that he has no true idea of God." It has taken all the philosophical and spiritual travail of the centuries to discover that there may be a concrete Infinite, an organic Absolute, an immanent Reality, and that the way to share in this comprehending Life is at least as much a way of affirmation as of negation, a way that leads not into "the Dark" but into the Light, and not into a "fathomless nothing," but into an abundant and radiant life.

Mysticism, as a type of religion, has further staked its precious realities too exclusively upon the functions of what to-day we call the subconscious. Impressed with the divine significance of "inward bubblings," the mystic has made too slight an account of the testimony of Reason and the contribution of History. The subconscious functions are very real and very important aspects of personal life, and can never again be ignored in any full account of personality. They influence every thought, feeling, attitude, volition, opinion, mood, and insight, and are thus operative in all the higher as well as in all the lower phases of human life and character. Metaphorically, but only metaphorically, we speak of the subconscious as a vast zone, an indefinable margin, surrounding the narrow focus of attention, and we may figuratively, but only figuratively, call it the subliminal "region" where all our life-gains, and often the gains of the race, are garnered. The contributions from this mental underworld are inestimable—we could not be men without them—but this subconscious zone is a source of things bad as well as good, things silly as well as things wise, of rubbish as well as of treasures, and it is diabolical as well as divine. It seems in rare moments to connect, as though it were a hidden inland stream, with the "immortal sea which brought us hither," and we feel at times, through its incomes, as though we were aware of *tides* from beyond our own margin. And, in fact, I believe we are.

But obviously we cannot assume that whatever comes

spontaneously out of the subconscious is divinely given. It mothers strange offspring—Esaus as well as Jacobs; its openings, its inrushes, its bubblings must be severely tested. Impulses of many sorts feel categorically imperative, but some call to deeds of light and some to deeds of darkness. They cannot be taken at their face value; they must be judged in some Court which is less capricious and which is guided by a more universal principle—something *semper et ubique*. A spiritual religion of the full and complete type will, I believe, have inward, mystical depth, it will keep vitalized and intensified with its experiences of divine supplies, and of union and unification with an environing Spirit, but it must at the same time soundly supplement its more or less capricious and subjective, and always fragmentary, mystical insights with the steady and unwavering testimony of Reason, and no less with the immense objective illumination of History.

The men whom I am here calling Spiritual Reformers are examples of this wider synthesis. They all read and loved the mystics and they themselves enjoyed times of direct refreshment from an inward Source of Life, but they were, most of them, at the same time, devoted Humanists. They shared with enthusiasm the rediscovery of those treasures which human Reason had produced, and they rose to a more virile confidence in the sphere and capacity of Reason than had prevailed in Christian circles since the days of the early Greek Fathers. They took a variety of roads to their conclusion, but in one way or another they all proclaimed that deep in the central nature of man—an inalienable part of Reason—there was a Light, a Word, an Image of God, something permanent, reliable, universal, and unsundered from God himself. They all knew that man is vastly more than "mere man." Hans Denck, one of the earliest of this group of Spiritual Reformers, declared that there is a *witness to God* in the soul of every man, and that without this inward Word it would be as impossible to bring men to God by outward means as it would be to show sunlight to eyeless men. He anticipated the great saying of Pascal in these words, "Apart from God no one can either seek or find God, for he who seeks God already in truth has Him."[18] "We are," says Jacob Boehme, who belongs in this line of Spiritual Reformers, "of God's substance: we have heaven and hell in ourselves."[19] There is in us, Peter Sterry says, a *unity of spirit* which holds all things together in an *at-once* experience, "a spire-top of spirit where all things meet and sit recollected and concentred in an unfathomed Depth of Life."[20] Most of these men were in revolt against scholasticism and all its works. They speak often very slightingly of "Reasoning," the attempt to find a way to ultimate Realities by logical syllogisms, but they, nevertheless, believed great things of man's rational and moral nature. They are often confused and cloudy in their explicit accounts of this ultimate moral and rational nature. They everywhere indicate the conceptual limitations under which even those who were the most emancipated from tradition were compelled to do their thinking in that age. They could not break the age-long spell and mighty fascination with which the Adam story and the Garden of Eden picture had held the Christian world. They were convinced, however, that the Augustinian interpretation of the fall, with its entail of an indelible taint upon the race forever, was an inadequate, if not an untrue account, though they could not quite arrive at an insight which enabled them to speak with authority on the fundamental nature of man. But with an instinct that pointed right, they took Adam as a type of the unspoiled man, and they saw writ large in him the possibilities and potentialities of man. What had been originally possible in Adam became, according to their thought, actual realization in Jesus Christ—the form and type of man, the true Head of the race—and in spite of the havoc and spoiling which sin had wrought, that original possibility, that divine potentiality, still reappears in every child, who comes now, as Adam did, made in the image of God, with the breath of God in him, and with creative freedom of will to settle his own destiny. Some of the Reformers whom I am here studying centre this image of God, this immense divine potentiality, in the ideal man, in man as God

conceives him in his perfect state, or as God by His Grace
intends him to be, and they do not go the whole bold way of
asserting that this man we know, this man who lives in time
and space, who loves and sins and suffers, has and always has,
in the very structure of his inmost moral and rational being, a
divine, unlost, inalienable, soul-centre which is unsundered
from God, and bears eternal witness to our origin from Him,
our potential likeness to Him, and our capacity to receive
illumination from Him.[21] But this latter bolder view of the
inherent greatness of man's essential nature is the prevailing
tendency of these men. They are thus the forerunners of the
Quaker faith that there is something of God in man, and they
continue the direct line, which goes back for ancestry to the
Socratic movement in philosophy of those who find God involved and implicated in the nature of normal self-consciousness and in the idea of the Good toward which we live.[22]

Mystics and prophets, as Seely well says in *Ecce Homo*, seem
to themselves to "discover truth not so much by a process of
reasoning as by *an intense gaze*, and they announce their conclusions with the voice of a herald, using the name of God
and giving no reasons." The rational way of approach is
different. It seeks to draw out by a process of rational argu-
ment what is involved in the outer or inner facts that are
present to consciousness. It does not claim the power to make
bricks without clay, to construct its conclusions out of nothing. Its only legitimate field is that of interpreting experience.
There have always been men who were religious because they
could not help being religious, because a Universe without
God seemed to them utterly irrational and unthinkable.
Schleiermacher is only one witness in a long and impressive
succession of thinkers that have insisted that "consciousness
of God and self-consciousness are inseparable."[23] It is obvious
even to the unmetaphysical person that self-consciousness
always presupposes and involves something prior to one's own
existence and some reality transcending the reality of one's
own self. The finite is intelligible only through the infinite,
the temporal only through the eternal. We cannot think at

all without appealing to some *permanent more of reality* than is just now given in our particular finite experience, and no matter how far one travels on the road of knowledge one always finds it still necessary to make reference to *a transcending more*. "All consciousness is," as Hegel showed in 1807, in his philosophical Pilgrim's Progress, the *Phenomenology of Spirit*, "an appeal to more consciousness," and there is no rational halting-place short of a self-consistent and self-explanatory spiritual Reality, which explains the origin and furnishes the goal of all that is real.

On the other hand, there have always been men who have not granted any such compelling implications to self-consciousness. They have maintained that "finites" are forever "finites," and that there are no bridges that carry us from our finite "nows" and "heres" to an infinite Reality. The infinite Reality, they all admit, is conceivable; it is "an idea" to which any mind can rise by normal processes of thought, "but," so they say, "an *idea* of an infinite Reality, an Infinite merely conceived in the mind, is different, by the whole width of the sky, from an actual objective infinite Reality that is *there*, and that contains inherently all that our hearts seek in God."

It is quite true, of course, that the presence of "an idea" in our mind does not of itself prove the existence of a corresponding objective reality *out there* in a world independent of our mind. There is most assuredly no way of bridging "the chasm" between mind and an objective world beyond and outside of mind, when once the "chasm" is assumed. But the fundamental error lies in the assumption of any such "chasm." The "chasm" which yawns between the inner and outer world is of our own making. Whenever we know anything, wherever there is knowledge at all, there is a synthetic indivisible whole of experience in which a subject knows an object. Subject and object cannot be really sundered without putting an instant end to knowledge—leaving "a bare grin without a face!" The only way we know anything is that we know we know it in experience. We do not ever succeed in proving that objects exist *out there* in the world beyond us exactly correspondent to these ideas in our minds. That is a feat of mental gymnastics quite parallel to that of "finding" the self with which we do the seeking. The crucial problem of knowledge is not to discover a bridge to leap the chasm between the mind within and the world beyond. It is rather the problem of finding a basis of verifying and testing what we know, and of making knowledge a consistent rational whole.

The method of testing and verifying any fact of truth which we have on our hands, is always to organize it and link it into a larger whole of knowledge which we ourselves, or the wider group of persons in which we are organic members, have verified, and to see that it fits in consistently into this larger whole, and in this rational process we always assume, and are bound to assume, some sort of Reality that transcends the fleeting and temporal, the caprice of the moment, the will of the subject, the here and the now. The mind that knows and knows that it knows must, as Plato centuries ago declared, rise from the welter and flux of momentary seemings to true Being, to the eternally Real,[24] and the knowledge process of binding fragments of experience into larger wholes and of getting articulate insight into the significance of many facts grasped in synthetic unity—in the "spire-top of spirit," as Sterry puts it—carries the mind steadily and irresistibly on to an infinitely-inclusive and self-explanatory spiritual Whole, which is always implied in knowledge. Some reference to the *permanent* is necessary in judging even the fleetingness of the "now," some confidence in the eternally true is essential for any pronouncement upon the false, some assurance of the infinite is presupposed in the endless dissatisfaction with the finite, some appeal to a total whole of Reality is implicated in any assertion that *this fact here and now* is known as real. Any one who feels the full significance of what is involved in knowing the *truth* has a coercive feeling that Eternity has been set within us, that our finite life is deeply rooted in the all-pervading Infinite.

The great thinkers of the first rank who have undertaken

to sound the significance of rational knowledge, and who have appreciated the meaning of the synthetic unity of the knowing mind and the world of objects that submit to its forms of thought, have recognized that there must be some deep-lying fundamental relation between the mind that knows and the world that is known, some Reality common to both outer and inner realms. They have, almost without exception, found themselves carried along irresistibly to an ultimate Reality that is the ground and explanation of all the fragmentary facts of experience, and without which nothing can be held to be permanent or rational—

> Something far more deeply interfused,
> Whose dwelling is the light of setting suns,
> And the round ocean and the living air,
> And the blue sky, and in the mind of man;
> A motion and a spirit, that impels
> All thinking things, all objects of all thought,
> And rolls through all things.[25]

The technical logical formulation of arguments to *prove* the existence of God as objectively real—arguments from causality, ontological arguments, and arguments from design—all of which assume a "chasm" between the knower and the object known, seem to us perhaps on critical analysis thin and insufficient. The bridge of formal logic seems too weak to carry us safely over from a finite here to an infinite yonder, from a contingent fact to an Absolute Reality, from something given *in* consciousness to Something existent outside and beyond it; but it is an impressive and significant fact that all finite experience, both of inner and outer events, involves a More yet, that we cannot think finite and contingent things without rational appeal to Something infinite and necessary, that human experience cannot be rationally conceived except as a fragment of a vastly more inclusive Experience, always recognized within the finite spirit, that unifies and binds together into one self-explanatory whole all that is absolutely Real and True, and this is Reason's conviction of God.

When once the conviction is *felt* and the rational postulate of God is made, it immediately verifies its practical value in the solution of our deepest problems. A happy illustration of the practical value and verifying evidence of the rational postulate of God has been given by James Ward: "Suppose," he says, "that the earth were wrapt in clouds all day while the sky was clear at night, so that we were able to see the planets and observe their movements as we do now, though the sun itself was invisible. The best account we could give of the planetary motions would still be to refer them to what for us, in accordance with our supposition, would only be an imaginary focus [or centre of physical energy], but one to which was assigned a position identical with the sun's [present] position."[26] This assumption would at once unlock the mystery and account for the varying movements of these visible bodies and the more rigorously the hypothesis were applied, the more exactly it would verify itself. So, too, with Reason's sublime venture of faith. The nature of self-consciousness demands the postulate, and once it is made it *works*.

The same result follows any attempt adequately to account for the moral imperative—the will to live the truly good life. The moral will turns out always to be imbedded in a deeper, richer, more inclusive Life than that of the fragmentary finite individual. There is a creative and autonomous central self in us which puts before us ideals of truth and beauty and goodness that are nowhere to be "found" in this world of sense-facts, and that yet are more real and august than any things our eyes see or our hands handle. Our main moral problem is not to adjust our inner ideals to our environment, but rather to compel the environment to level up to our ideals. The world that ought to be makes us forever dissatisfied with the world that is, and sets us with a fixity of purpose at the task of realizing the Kingdom which might possibly be, which we know ought to be, and which, therefore, has our loyal endeavour that it shall be, regardless of the cost in pain and sacrifice. Man, as William Wallace has put it, "projects his own self-to-be into the nature he seeks to conquer. Like an assailant who should succeed in throwing his standard into the strong central keep of the enemy's fortress, and fight his way thereto with assured victory in his eyes of hope, so man with the vision of his soul prognosticates his final triumph."[27] But if the life of moral endeavour is to be essentially consistent and reasonable there must be a world of Reality that transcends this realm of empirical, causal, and utilitarian happenings. Struggle for ends of goodness must be at least as significant in function as struggle for existence; our passion for what ought to be must have had birth in an inner eternal environment at least as real as that which produced our instincts and appetite for the things by which we live in time. If the universe is through and through rational, there must be some personal Heart that *cares;* some moral Will that guarantees and backs our painful strivings—our groaning and travailing—to make what ought to be come into play here in the world which is. This postulate is Reason's faith in God, and again it *works.*

The evolution of life—if it is evolving as we believe it is, and if it is to be viewed with rational insight as an upward process—irresistibly involves and implies some sort of fundamental intelligence and conscious purpose, some Logos steering the mighty movement. We have outgrown crude arguments from "design," and we cannot think of God as a foreign and external Creator, working as a Potter on his clay; but it is irrational to "explain" a steadily unfolding movement, an ever-heightening procession of life, by "fortuitous variations," by "accidental" shifts of level, or even by a blind *élan vital.* If there is an increasing purpose and a clearly culminating drama unfolding in this moving flood of life, then there is some Mind that sees the way, and some Will that directs the march of Life. And this confidence of ours in some divine Event to which the whole creation moves, this insight that there must be a significant and adequate explanation for the immanent teleology and beauty with which our universe is crammed, is, once more, Reason's postulate of God. There is something in us, indissoluble from Reason itself—a

Light, a Word, a Witness as these Spiritual Reformers insisted
—which links us in all the deeper processes of self-consciousness with *That Which Is* and without which "knowledge"
would be a mere flux of seemings, a flight of *seriatim* items.

> When this world's pleasures for my soul sufficed,
> Ere my heart's plummet sounded depths of pain,
> I called on reason to control my brain,
> And scoffed at that old story of the Christ.
>
> But when o'er burning wastes my feet had trod,
> And all my life was desolate with loss,
> With bleeding hands I clung about the cross,
> And cried aloud, "Man needs a suffering God."[28]

There can be no doubt that the compulsions and implications of rational insight have brought multitudes of men to
God, have given them an unescapable conviction of His
reality, and have swayed their wills to live in conformity to
His perfect Goodness; and it is also true that when for any
cause this clue of rationality is missed or lost, men flounder
about in the fog and pass through periods of inward tragedy
amounting often to despair. But the approach of Reason still
leaves much to be desired. It points to something deeper than
the transitory flux of things, it raises our minds to some sort
of ultimate and self-explanatory Reality, it compels the conviction that there is an all-inclusive Logos—Mind or Spirit—
that explains what is and what ought to be, and what in the
unfolding course of things is to be; but it does not bring us to
a personal God who is our loving Friend and the intimate
Companion of our souls, it does not help us solve the mystery
of human suffering that lies heavily upon our lives, and it
does not bring to our spirits *the saving reinforcement of personal
Love* that must be a central feature of a spiritual and adequate
religion.

There is still another way of approach to a Religion for
mature minds which has been no less universally operative

and no less dynamic in its transforming effects upon human lives than either of the two tendencies so far considered—I refer to the way of Faith. By Faith I mean the soul's moral or appreciative apprehension of God as *historically revealed*, particularly as revealed in the personal life of Jesus Christ. This Faith-way to God cannot be wholly separated—except by an artificial abstraction—from the inward way of mysticism, or from the implications of Reason. It is no blind acceptance of traditional opinions, no uncritical reliance on "authority," or on some mysterious infallible oracle. It is the spiritual response—or "assent," as Clement of Alexandria called it—the moral swing of our inmost self, as we catch insights of a loving Heart and holy Will revealed through the words and lives and sufferings of saints and prophets, who have lived by their vision of God, and supremely revealed in the Life and Love, the Passion and the Triumphs of that Person whose experience and character and incarnation of life's possibilities seem at last adequate for all the needs—the heights and the depths—of this complex life of ours.

It was Luther's living word which first brought the momentous significance of Faith to clear consciousness in the sixteenth century. But the new way of Faith meant many and discordant things, according to the preparation of the ears of those who heard. It spoke, as all Pentecosts do, to each man in his own tongue. To those who came to the Lutheran insight with a deep hunger of spirit for reality and with minds liberated by Humanistic studies, the Faith-message meant new heavens and a new earth. It was a new discovery of God, and a new estimate of man. They suddenly caught a vision of life as it was capable of becoming, and they committed their fortunes to the task of making that possible world real. By a shift of view, as revolutionary as that from Ptolemaic astronomy to the verifiable insight of Copernicus, they passed over from the dogma of a Christ who came to appease an angry God, and to found a Church as an ark of safety in a doomed world, to the living apprehension of a Christ—verifiable in experience—who revealed to them, in terms of His own nature, an eternally tender, loving, suffering, self-giving God, and who made them see, with the enlightened eyes of their heart, the divine possibilities of human life. Through this insight, they were the beginners of a new type of Christianity, which has become wide-spread and impressive in the modern world, a type that finds the supreme significance of Christ's Life in His double revelation of the inherent nature of God, and the immense value and potentiality of man, and that changes the emphasis from schemes of salvation to interpretations of life, from the magic significance of doctrine to the incalculable worth of the moral will.

These men were weak in historical sense, and, like everybody else in their generation, they used Scripture without much critical insight. But they hit upon a principle which saved them from slavery to texts, and which gave them a working faith in the steady moral and spiritual development of man. I mean the principle that this Christ whom they had discovered anew was an eternal manifestation of God, an immanent Word of God, a Spirit brooding over the world of men, as in the beginning over the face of the waters, present in the unfolding events of history as well as in the far-away "dispensations of Grace." As a result, they grew less interested in the problem that had fascinated so many mystics, the problem of the super-empirical evolution of the divine Consciousness; the super-temporal differentiation of the unity of the Godhead into a Father and Son and self-revealing Holy Ghost; and they tried rather to appreciate and to declare the concrete revelation through Christ, and the import of His visible and invisible presence in the world.[29]

This approach of Faith, this appreciation of the nature of God as He has been unveiled in the ethical processes of history, especially in the Person of Christ, and in His expanding conquest of the world, must always be one of the great factors of spiritual religion. The profound results of higher criticism, with its stern winnowings, have brought us face to face with problems unknown to the sixteenth and seventeenth centuries. So much of what seemed the solid continent of historical truth has weathered and crumbled away that some have wondered whether any irreducible nucleus would remain firm and permanent above the flood of the years, and whether the religion of the future must not dispense with the historical element, and the Faith-aspect that goes with it, and rest wholly upon present inward experience.

There are, however, I believe, no indications worth considering, of the disappearance of Jesus Christ from human history. On the contrary, He holds, as never before, the commanding place in history. He still dominates conscience, by the moral sway of His Life of Goodness, as does no other person who has ever lived; and by the attractive power of His life and love He still sets men to living counter to the strong thrust of instinct and impulse as does no one else who has ever touched the springs of conduct. The Faith-aspect is still a very live element in religion, and it is, as it has been so often before, precisely the aspect which supplies concrete body and filling and objective ethical direction to our deep subconscious yearnings and strivings and experiences.

Once at least there shone through the thin veil of matter a personal Life which brought another kind of world than this world of natural law and utilitarian aims full into light. There broke through here in the face of Jesus Christ a revelation of purpose in the universe so far beyond the vague trend of purpose dimly felt in slowly evolving life that it is possible here to catch an illuminating vision of what the goal of the long drama may be—the unveiling of sons of God. Here the discovery can be made that the deepest Reality toward which Reason points, and which the mystical experience *feels*, is no vague Something Beyond, but a living, loving Some One, dealing with us as Person with person. In Him there comes to focus in a Life that we can love and appreciate a personal character which impresses us as being absolutely good, and as being in its inexhaustible depth of Love and Grace worthy to be taken as the revelation of the true nature of the God whom all human hearts long for. And finally through this personal revelation of God in Christ there has come to us a clear insight that pain and suffering and tragedy can be taken up into a self-chosen Life and absorbed without spoiling its immense joy, and that precisely through suffering-love, joyously accepted, a Person expressing in the world the heart of God may become the moral and spiritual Saviour of others. As von Hügel has finely said: "A Person came and lived and loved, and did and taught, and died and rose again, and lives on by His power and His Spirit forever within us and amongst us, so unspeakably rich and yet so simple, so sublime and yet so homely, so divinely above us precisely in being so divinely near that His character and teaching require, for an ever fuller yet never complete understanding, the varying study, and different experiments and applications, embodiments and unrollings of all the races and civilizations, of all the individual and corporate, the simultaneous and successive experiences of the human race to the end of time."[30]

The only salvation worth talking about is that which consists of an inner process of moral transformation, through which one passes over "the great divide" from a life that is self-centred and dominated by impulse and sin to a life that is assured of divine forgiveness, that has conceived a passion for a redeemed inward nature, that is conscious of help from beyond its own resources, and that is dedicated to the task of making moral goodness triumph over the evil of the world. Any experience which brings to the soul a clear vision of the moral significance of human life, and that engenders in us a practical certainty that God is working with us in all our deepest undertakings, tends to have saving efficacy and to bring about this inward transformation. But nowhere else in the universe—above us or within us—has the moral significance of life come so full into sight, or the reality of actual divine fellowship, whether in our aspirations or in our failures, been raised to such a pitch of practical certainty as in the personal life and death and resurrection and steady historical triumph of Jesus Christ. He exhibits in living fulness, with transforming power, a Life which consciously felt itself one with the heart and will of God. He reveals the inherent blessedness of Love—even though it may involve suffering and pain and death. He shows the moral supremacy, even in this imperfect empirical world, of the perfectly good will, and He impresses those who *see* Him—see Him, I mean, with eyes that can penetrate through the temporal to the eternal and find His real nature—as being the supreme personal unveiling of God, as worthy to be our Leader, our Ideal Life, our typical personal Character, and strong enough in His infinite Grace and divine self-giving to convince us of the eternal co-operation of God with our struggling humanity, and to settle our Faith in the essential Saviourhood of God.

He who sees *that* in Christ has found a real way to God and has discovered a genuine way of salvation. It is the way of Faith, but Faith is no airy and unsubstantial road, no capricious leap. There is no kind of aimful living conceivable that does not involve faith in something trans-subjective— faith in something not given in present empirical experience. Even in our most elementary life-adjustments there is something operative in us which far underlies our conscious perceiving and the logic of our conclusions. We are moved, not alone by what we clearly picture and coldly analyse, but by deep-lying instincts which defy analysis, by background and foreground fringes of consciousness, by immanent and penetrative intelligence which cannot be brought to definite focus, by the vast reservoirs of accumulated wisdom through which we *feel* the way to go, though we can pictorially envisage no "spotted trees" that mark the trail.

This religious and saving Faith, through which the soul discovers God and makes the supreme life-adjustment to Him, is profoundly moral and, in the best sense of the word, rational. It does not begin with an assumption, blind or otherwise, as to Christ's metaphysical nature, it does not depend upon the adoption of systematically formulated doctrines; it becomes operative through the discovery of a personal Life, historically lived—and continued through the centuries as a transforming Spirit—rich enough in its experience to exhibit the infinite significance of life, inwardly deep enough in its

spiritual resources to reveal the character of God, and strong
enough in sympathy, in tenderness, in patience, and in self-
giving love to beget forever trust and confidence and love on
the part of all who thus find Him.

The God whom we learn to know in Christ—the God historically revealed—is no vague first Cause, no abstract Reality,
no all-negating Absolute. He is a concrete Person, whose traits
of character are intensely moral and spiritual. His will is no
fateful swing of mechanical law; it is a morally good will
which works patiently and forever toward a harmonized
world, a Kingdom of God. The central trait of His character
is love. He does not *become* Father, He is not reconciled to us
by persuasive offerings and sacrifices. He is inherently and by
essential disposition Father and the God of all Grace. He is
not remote and absentee—making a world "in the beginning,"
and leaving it to run by law, or only occasionally interrupting
its normal processes—He is immanent Spirit, working always,
the God of beauty and organizing purpose. He is Life and
Light and Truth, an Immanuel God who can and does show
Himself in a personal Incarnation, and so exhibits the course
and goal of the race. The way of Faith is a way to God, and
the religion of this type is as properly *a first-hand religion* as
that of any other type.

I have, of course, by no means exhausted the types of
mature religion. There are other ways of approach to God,
other roads by which the soul finds the way home—"On the
East three gates; on the North three gates; on the South three
gates; and on the West three gates"—and they will continue
to be sacred ways—*viae sacrae*—for those who travel them and
thus find their heart's desire. What we should learn from this
brief study is that religion is too rich and complex an experience to be squeezed down to some one isolated aspect of life
or of consciousness. There are many ways to God and any
way that actually brings the soul to Him is a good way, but
the best way is that one which produces upon the imperfect
personal life the profoundest saving effects, the most dynamic
moral reinforcement, and which brings into sway over the

will the goal of life most adequate for men like us in a social world like ours.

For most of us no one way of approach—no single type of religion—is quite sufficient for all the needs of our life. Most of us are fortunate enough to have at least moments when we feel in warm and intimate *contact* with a divine, enwrapping environment more real to us than things of sense and of arithmetic, and when the infinite and eternal is no less, but immeasurably more, sure than the finite and temporal. Most of us, again, succeed, at least on happy occasions of mental health, in finding rational clues which carry us through the maze of contingency and clock-time happenings, through the imperfections of our slow successive events, to the One Great Now of perfect Reality which explains the process, and we attain to an intellectual love of God. And in spite of the literary difficulties of primitive narratives and of false trails which the historical Church has again and again taken, almost any serious, earnest soul to-day may find that divine Face, that infinitely deep and luminous Personality who spoke as no man ever spake, who loved as none other ever loved, who saw more in humanity than anybody else has ever seen, and who felt as no other person ever has that He was one in heart and mind and will with God; and having found Him, by a morally responsive Faith which dominates and transforms the inward self, one has found God as Companion, Friend, and Saviour. Where all these ways converge, and a soul enjoys the privilege of mystical contact, the compulsion of rational insight, and the moral reinforcement of personal Faith in Christ, religion comes to its consummate flower, and may with some right be called "spiritual religion."

The most radical step which these spiritual Reformers took —the step which put them most strikingly out of line with the main course of the Reformation—was their break with Protestant Theology. They were not satisfied with a programme which limited itself to a correction of abuses, an abolition of mediaeval superstitions, and a shift of external authority. They were determined to go the whole way to a religion of inward life and power, to a Christianity whose only authority should be its dynamic and spiritual authority. They placed as low an estimate on the saving value of orthodox systems of theological formulation as the Protestant Reformers did on the saving value of "works." To the former, salvation was an affair neither of "works" nor of what they called "notions," *i.e.* views, beliefs, or creeds. They are never weary of insisting that a person may go on endless pilgrimages to holy places, he may repeat unnumbered "paternosters," he may mortify his body to the verge of self-destruction, and still be unsaved and unspiritual; so, too, he may "believe" all the dogma of the most orthodox system of faith, he may take on his lips the most sacred words of sound doctrine, and yet be utterly alien to the kingdom of God, a stranger and a foreigner to the spirit of Christ. They were determined, therefore, to go through to a deeper centre and to make only those things pivotal which are absolutely essential to life and salvation.

They began their reconstruction of the meaning of salvation with (1) a new and fresh interpretation of God, and (2) with a transformed eschatology. As I have already said, they rediscovered God through Christ, and in terms of His revelation; and coming to God *this way*, they saw at once that the prevailing interpretations of the atonement were inadequate and unworthy. God, they declared, is not a Suzerain, treating men as his vassals, reckoning their sins up against them as infinite debts to be paid off at last in a vast commercial transaction only by the immeasurable price of a divine Life, given to pay the debt which had involved the entire race in hopeless bankruptcy. Nor, again, in their thought is He a mighty Sovereign, meting out to the world strict justice and holding all sin as flagrant disloyalty and appalling violation of law, never to be forgiven until the full requirements of sovereign justice are met and balanced and satisfied. All this seemed to them artificial and false. Salvation, as they understand it, cannot be conceived as escape from debt nor as the satisfaction of justice, since it is a personal life-relationship with a personal God who is and always was eternal Love. God's universe, both outer and inner, is loaded with moral significance, is meant for discipline, and therefore it has its stern aspects and drives its lessons home with the unswerving hammer of *consequences*. But in the personal Heart of the universe, Love and Tenderness and Sympathy and Forgiveness are supreme, and every process and every instrument of salvation, in the divine purpose, is vital, ethical, spiritual.

God has shown Himself as Father. He has revealed the immeasurable suffering which sin inflicts on love. To find the Father-Heart; to cry "Abba" in filial joy; to die to sin and to be born to love, is to be saved. Jacob Boehme gave this new conception of God, and its bearing on the way of salvation, the most adequate expression that was given by any of this group, but all these so-called spiritual Reformers herein studied had reached the same insight at different levels of adequacy. Their return to a more vital conception of salvation, with its emphasis on the value of personality, brought with it, too, a new humanitarian spirit and a truer estimate of the worth of man. As they re-discovered the love of God, they also found again the gospel of love and brotherhood which is woven into the very tissue of the original gospel of divine Fatherhood.

Their revised eschatology was due, at least partly, to this altered account of the character of God, but it was also partly due to their profound tendency to deal with all matters of the soul in terms of life and vital processes. Heaven and Hell were no longer thought of as terminal places, where the saved were everlastingly rewarded and the lost forever punished. Heaven and Hell were for them inward conditions, states of the soul, the normal gravitation of the Spirit toward its chosen centre. Heaven and Hell cease, therefore, to be eschatological in the true sense of the word; they become present realities, tendencies of life, ways of reacting toward the things of deepest import. Heaven, whether here or in any other world, is the condition of complete adjustment to the holy will of God; it is joy in the prevalence of His goodness; peace through harmonious correspondence with His purposes; the formation of a spirit of love, the creation of an inward nature that loves what God loves and enjoys what He enjoys.

Hell, here or elsewhere, is a disordered life, out of adjustment with the universal will of God; it is concentration upon self and self-ends; the contraction of love; the shrinking of inward resources; the formation of a spirit of hate, the creation of an inward nature that hates what God loves. Hell is the inner condition inherently attaching to the kind of life that displays and exhibits the spirit and attitude which must be overcome before God with His purposes of goodness can be ultimately triumphant and all in all. Salvation, therefore, cannot be thought of in terms of escape from a place that is dreaded to a place that is desired as a haven. It is through and through a spiritual process—escape from a wrongly fashioned will to a will rightly fashioned. It is complete spiritual health and wholeness of life, brought into operation and function by the soul's recovery of God and by joyous correspondence with Him.

Here is the genuine beginning in modern times of what has come to be the deepest note of present-day Christianity, *the appreciation of personality as the highest thing in earth or heaven*, and the initiation of a movement to find the vital sources and resources for the inner kindling of the spirit, and for raising the whole personal life to higher functions and to higher powers.

Putting the emphasis, as they did, on personal religion, *i.e.* on experience, instead of on theology, they naturally became exponents of free-will, and that, too, in a period when foreordination was a central dogma of theology. This problem of freedom, which is as deep as personality itself, always has its answer "determined" by the point of approach. For those who *begin* with an absolute and omnipotent God, and work down from above, the necessarian position is determined. Their answer is: "All events are infallibly connected with God's disposal." For those who start, however, from actual experience and from the testimony of consciousness, freedom feels as certain as life itself. Their answer is: "Human will is a real factor in the direction of events and man shapes his own destiny toward good or evil." Calvin's logic is irresistible if his assumptions are once granted. These spiritual Reformers, however, were untouched by it, because they began from the interior life, with its dramatic movements, as their basic fact, and man as they knew him was free.

This spiritual movement involved, as a natural development, an entire shift from the historical idea of the Church as an authoritative and supernatural instrument of salvation, to a Church whose authority was entirely vital, ethical, spiritual, dynamic. The Church of these spiritual Reformers was a Fellowship, a Society, a Family, rather than a mysterious and supernatural entity. They felt once again, as powerfully perhaps as it was possible in their centuries to feel it, the immense significance of the Pauline conception of the Church as the continued embodiment and revelation of Christ, the communion of saints past and present who live or have lived by the Spirit. Through this spiritual group, part of whom are visible and part invisible, they held that the divine revelation is continued and the eternal Word of God is being uttered to the race. "The true religion of Christ," as one of these spiritual teachers well puts it, "is written in the soul and spirit of man by the Spirit of God; and the believer is the only book in which God now writes His New Testament."[31] This Church of the Spirit is always being built. Its power is proportional to the spiritual vitality of the membership, to the measure of apprehension of divine resources, to the depth of insight and grasp of truth, to the prevalence of love and brotherhood, to the character of service, which the members exhibit. It possesses no other kind of power or authority than the power and authority of personal lives formed into a community by living correspondence with God, and acting as human channels and organs of His Life and Spirit. Such a Church can meet new formulations of science and history and social ideals with no authoritative and conclusive word of God which automatically settles the issue. Its only weapons are truth and light, and these have to be continually re-discovered and re-fashioned to fit the facts which the age has found and verified. Its mission is *prophetic*. It does not dogmatically decide what facts must be believed, but it sees and announces the spiritual significance of the facts that are discovered and verified. It was, thus, in their thought a growing, changing, ever-adjusting body—the living body of Christ in the world. To the Protestant Reformers this spiritual ideal presented "a Church" so shorn and emasculated as to be absolutely worthless. It seemed to them a propaganda which threatened and endangered the mighty work of reformation to which they felt themselves called, and they used all the forces available to suppress and annihilate those of this other "way."

Nearly four hundred wonderful years have passed since the issue was first drawn, since the first of these spiritual prophets uttered his modest challenge. There can be no question that the current of Christian thought has been strongly setting in the direction which these brave and sincere innovators took. I feel confident that many persons to-day will be interested in these lonely men and will follow with sympathy their valiant struggles to discover the road to a genuine spiritual religion, and their efforts to live by the eternal Word of God as it was freely revealed as the Day Star to their souls.

NOTES

1. 1 Cor. xv. 50.
2. 2 Cor. v. 1–4.
3. John iii. 6.
4. 1 John iv. 13; John xiii. 34 and xvi. 13; 1 John iv. 4.
5. They found their authority for this outer sheath of body in the text which says: "The Lord God made for Adam and for his wife coats of skins, and clothed them."—Gen. iii. 21.
6. Many of these historical reappearances are considered in my *Studies in Mystical Religion*.
7. Isaac Penington, "A True and Faithful Relation of my Spiritual Travails," *Works* (edition of 1761), i. pp. xxxvii.–xxxviii.
8. Isaac Penington's *Works*, loc. cit.
9. The exact and sharply-defined "ladders" of mystic ascent which form a large part of the descriptive material in books on Mystical Religion are far from being universal ladders. Like creeds, or like religious institutions,

they powerfully assist certain minds to find the way home, but they seem unreal and artificial to many other persons, and they must be considered only as symbolisms which speak to the condition of a limited number of spiritual pilgrims.

10. Wordsworth's "Prelude," Bk. ii.
11. *Theologia Germanica*, chaps. xxii. and xliii.
12. *Ibid.* chap. liii.
13. *Meister Eckhart*, Pfeiffer, p. 320. 20.
14. Tauler's Sermons. See especially Sermons IV. and XXIII. in Hutton's *Inner Way*.
15. *The Divine Names* of Dionysius the Areopagite, chap. i. sec. i.
16. *Meister Eckhart*, Pfeiffer, p. 320. 25–30.
17. Quoted in W. H. J. Gairdner's *The Reproach of Islam*, p. 151.
18. Denck's *Was geredet sey, dass die Schrift*, B. 2. Pascal's saying is: "Comfort thyself; thou wouldst not be seeking Me hadst thou not already found Me."—*Le Mystère de Jésus*, sec. 2.
19. *The Threefold Life of Man*, xiv. 72.
20. Sterry's *Rise, Race, and Royalty of the Kingdom of God in the Soul of Man*, p. 24.
21. "The finite individual soul seems naturally to present a double aspect. It looks like, on the one hand, a climax or concentration of the nature beneath it and the community around it, and, on the other hand, a spark or fragment from what is above and beyond it. It is crystallized out of the collective soul of nature or society, or it falls down from the transcendental soul of heaven or what is above humanity. In both cases alike it has its share of divinity."—Bernard Bosanquet, *The Value and Destiny of the Individual* (London, 1913), p. 1.
22. The way to the world of Perfect Reality, Socrates says in the *Theaetetus*, consists in likeness to God, nor is there, he adds, anything more like God than is a good man.—*Theaetetus* 176 A and B.
23. Schleiermacher's *Glaubenslehre*.
24. *Republic* vii. 518 B.
25. Wordsworth's "Tintern Abbey."
26. *Realm of Ends*, p. 230.
27. *Lectures and Addresses*, p. 193.
28. Ella Wheeler Wilcox, *Poems of Life and Moments*.
29. Jacob Boehme, however, shows this fascination for the super-empirical at its height and culmination. It was an attempt, though a bungling attempt, to pass from an abstract God to a God of *character*, and it was a circuitous way of getting round the problem of evil.
30. *Mystical Elements of Religion*, i. p. 26.
31. William Dell's sermon on "The Trial of Spirits," *Works*, p. 438.

3

The Beginnings of Quakerism

THE researches of recent years conclusively show that the movement, known in history as Quakerism, was part of a very much wider religious movement which had for many years been gathering volume and intensity, and which had prepared the way, especially in England, for this particular type of lay-religion. I have endeavoured to trace, in my *Studies in Mystical Religion*, one powerful line of influences which helped to form the religious sects of the Commonwealth period and the peculiar religious atmosphere which prevailed at that time. I am now engaged upon a second volume of *Studies*,[1] which will, I hope, trace out other great lines of formative influence, and make much clearer than heretofore the spiritual conditions and environment of that creative epoch in which Quakerism was born.

It is not yet, and probably will not ever be, possible to prove that George Fox and the other leaders of this special movement *consciously* adopted their ideas and methods, their peculiar testimonies and form of organization, from the Separatist sects which swarmed about them, and which were the product of many centuries of striving after an inward way to God. George Fox was not a reader of books other than the Bible, nor a student of movements, and he reveals in his writings very slight direct acquaintance with the formative literature of mystical religion. This is true also of Dewsbury, Nayler, Howgill, Burrough, and the other early makers of Quakerism. They one and all, as we shall see, trace their inspiration and their constructive ideas to direct Divine "openings," and they believed that they were being led as God guides the bird, along a trackless way.

We know that George Fox, through his uncle Pickering,

had some personal connection with the Anabaptists, and that again in 1647 he came into religious fellowship with a company of Baptists in Nottinghamshire.[2] Throughout his period of travail and discovery he came in close contact with the small sects, and shared their fervent desire for an inward religion. We also know that Dewsbury and many of the other secondary leaders were in intimate connection with the Seekers and other separate groups, and it is evident that this connection had a formative influence upon the Quaker movement, though the leaders themselves were apparently not aware that they were drawing their water from any earthly cisterns, and thought sincerely enough that the new type of religion which they were inaugurating was given to them by revelation. The marks of outside influence are, nevertheless, clearly apparent, and there are impressive evidences that they were unconsciously moulded and nurtured by the social environment and the intellectual climate in which they lived and breathed.

It is now well known that subconscious or unconscious imitation, and sympathetic assimilation of ideas by processes of suggestion, are the prime influences for the formation of the elemental disposition, the trend or tendency of the personal life, the deep-lying ground-swell of the character, the ideals which have their function below the level of thought. The influence of heredity is no doubt a powerful factor, but a very large part of the mental equipment, once attributed to inheritance, is more properly assigned to these profoundly shaping processes, suggestion and imitation, through which the new-born individual takes to himself the ideas, activities, manners, customs, emotional traits, strivings, and *spirit* of the group which most impresses his life.

It is through just these processes that the subconscious life is stored—the *heart*, to use the ancient terminology, is formed —and it is precisely because the formation has gone on below consciousness that the ideas and aims thus acquired often rise above the threshold suddenly, and burst into consciousness as though they had originated in another world. A new compartment of the self seems flung open by an unseen hand.

This is peculiarly the case with the type of persons who belong to the class of geniuses or creative leaders. They are always persons who are acutely sensitive to the spirit of their time, the subtle currents and inward strivings of their period. They are as responsive to group-tendencies as a sounding-box of a musical instrument to vibrations; they are *suggestible* to a degree that ordinary thick-skinned mortals have no notion of. Like Joan of Arc, they hear themselves summoned to missions though the air is stirred by the vibrations of no voices, and they find their minds possessed of truths for which they have paid fees to no human teacher. Furthermore, these highly sensitive souls are responsive not only to what I have called group-tendencies, but they appear also to be able to set themselves into parallelism with celestial currents, and to become sensitive organs of direct spiritual impressions and divine revelations which are missed by those who are busy alone with the affairs of time and sense.

The Commonwealth period abounded in persons of the acutely responsive type. Some of them were highly endowed, well organized, profoundly moral in purpose, and capable of being constructed by the new experiences and fresh ideas which came to them; others were loosely knit, easily disorganized, badly balanced, weak in moral stature, and therefore ready material for hysteria and dissociation when the stable order of ancient doctrine and practice was upset, and a flood of new ideas, loaded with emotional quality, seethed about them. Richard Baxter—a man both "highly endowed" and "well organized"—in his *Self-Review*, written toward the end of his life, gives a luminous account of the way in which he passed from the religion of "the unriper times of his youth"— when he had been opposed to these freer and more personal types of religion—to a religion inwardly experienced and grasped. "Had I been void of internal experience," he confesses, "and the adhesion of love, and the special help of God . . . I had certainly apostatized. I am, therefore, much more apprehensive than heretofore of the necessity of well grounding men in their

religion, and especially of the witness of the indwelling Spirit,
for the Spirit is the great witness of Christ and of Christianity
in the world." This direction in which Baxter moved was the
direction in which many great souls of that time were moving.
There were numerous persons, both outside and inside the
Quaker group, who, quite independently of George Fox, had
the "internal experience" and arrived at the insight that religion, to be true and spiritual, must be "well grounded in the
witness of the indwelling Spirit." But George Fox is nevertheless the genuine *prophet* of this fresh idea, the leader who
drew together into one unified movement aspects of truth
which were powerless while in abstraction. He exhibited very
unusual gifts of penetrating to the heart of the truth until it
possessed him, of putting it into practical expression in deeds,
of convicting other persons of his truth, and he had the genius
to exercise a leadership that profoundly affected every fol-
lower, and at the same time left full scope for almost complete
individual liberty and personal initiative and development.
His life and leadership are impressively and freshly presented
in the following chapters, and need no addition here. I shall
deal especially with the peculiar psychical traits in him which
must be taken into account before his life and work can be
adequately estimated.

Nobody who is equipped with a moderate amount of psychological knowledge can fail to discover in the *Journal* traces
of these "peculiar psychical traits." Although earlier readers
seldom or never noted the significance of the passages which
reveal Fox's extraordinary constitution, it is a fact that this
Journal is one of the best modern biographical accounts of a
personality, at once subject to profound transformations, occurring independently of the will and going on below the level
of consciousness—transformations deeply affecting the functions of body and mind—and at the same time a personality
possessed of rare moral and spiritual penetration, endowed
with marked traits of leadership, and capable of making—he
knew not how—an impressive contribution to the religious
progress of the race. A few concrete biographical instances

will indicate the type of experience to which I refer: "I went," he writes of himself during his long and agonizing voyage of discovery, "to one Macham, a priest in high account. And he would needs give me some physic, and I was to have been let blood; *but they could not get one drop of blood from me either in arms or head though they endeavoured to do so, my body being, as it were, dried up with sorrows, grief and troubles.*"[3] This vivid passage tells a plain story of a pathological condition well known to all students of psychology, and the various automatic movements, subliminal uprushes, and sudden suggestions which characterize this period of his life, as recorded in the *Journal*, all fit in well with his fundamental psychical condition.

Somewhat later a certain man named Brown "had great prophecies and sights upon his death-bed," and said that George Fox was to be an instrument of the Lord. "When this man was buried," the *Journal* says, "a great work of the Lord fell upon me, to the admiration [wonder] of many, who thought I had been dead: and many came to see me for about fourteen days' time for *I was very much altered in countenance and person, as if my body had been new-moulded or changed*. . . . I saw into that which was without end, and things which cannot be uttered."[4] Another experience of this sort occurred while George Fox was in Reading in 1659, when he saw that there was "great confusion and distraction amongst the people and that the powers were plucking each other to pieces." "I was there," he writes, "under great sufferings and exercises and in a great travail in my spirit for about ten weeks' time. . . . I had a sight and sense of the king's return. . . . While the great exercise was upon my spirit, my countenance was altered and I looked poor and thin."[5] He had a *vision*, probably at this time, in which he saw the city of London "lie in heaps and the gates down, just as I saw it several years after lying in heaps when it was burned."[6]

The most profound of these psychical experiences came upon him suddenly in 1670 as he was walking down a hill near Rochester. "A great weight and oppression," he says, "fell upon my spirit." "I was extremely loaden and burdened with the world's spirits that my life was oppressed under them." Finally he got to Stratford, where he "lay exceeding weak and at last lost both my hearing and my sight." While in this condition many persons came to see him, and though he could not see their persons, he says that he could "discern their spirits." Under "these sufferings and groanings and travails, and sorrows and oppressions," he lay for several weeks; few thought he could live, and a rumour even spread abroad that he was dead. The state of disturbance lasted many months with shifting experiences, all indicating serious pathological conditions. "I was," he says, "under great sufferings at this time beyond what I have words to declare, for I was brought into the deep, and saw all the religions of the world, and people that lived in them. . . . Whilst I was under this spiritual travail and suffering, the state of the city New Jerusalem which comes down out of heaven was opened to me."[7] These instances of profound transformation were correlated with external events and happenings of momentous significance. They were times when Fox was under heavy stress and strain and was subjected to unusual mental and emotional tension.

The sudden suggestive effect upon his mind of church or cathedral spires, especially in the early intense period of his life, is, again, very striking, and led on one occasion to the famous shoeless pilgrimage through the streets of Lichfield and the cry of warning, "Woe to the bloody city."[8] His extraordinary power of sitting in rapt silence for hours at a time is significant, and so too is the frequently mentioned power of his eyes.[9] There are many instances in his own account of instantaneous healings, wrought either upon himself or upon others. For example, in 1652 "a rude fellow, with a walking rule-staff," struck Fox with all his might a blow across his arm. The arm and hand were so bruised that he lost all power to move them, and the people cried out, "He hath spoiled his hand forever." "But," says Fox, "I looked at it in the love of God, and after a while the Lord's power sprang through me again, and through my hand and arm, so that in a moment I recovered strength in my hand and arm in the sight of them all."[10] There are, too, in his accounts a number of impressive telepathic experiences.

His psychical constitution was thus plainly of a very unstable sort, and if he had not found near the end of his adolescent period an organizing, centralizing, and constructive power, his story would have been vastly different. But fortunately he did find the centralizing power—"the key," as he calls it, "which opened life to me." Constructive energy swept into him as though a mountain reservoir of power had been tapped, and this youth, evidently marked with hysteria, whose blood would not flow, and who on occasion lost his sight and hearing, rose into a robust and virile man, "stiff as a tree and pure as a bell," ready to stand the world with its jeers, its blows, and its barbaric prisons; able to carry his message on foot or on horseback through England, Wales, Scotland, and Ireland, and to carry through an amazing Western missionary journey through Barbados and Jamaica, across to the shore of Maryland, up to the New England colonies, and back to the Carolinas; capable of exercising a transforming influence and power over such men as William Penn, Isaac Penington, and Robert Barclay; possessed of sufficient insight to organize a new type of religious society and to initiate far-reaching moral and social reforms; strong enough to stand flattery and adulation and the unexpected success of leadership, and profound enough in his interpretation of life to attract the attention of serious and thoughtful persons now for over two centuries and a half.

This extraordinary and seemingly abnormal aspect of Fox's early constitution must, however, not be considered in isolation and apart from certain other traits which were equally fundamental to his nature. He was, he says, from his early childhood marked by "gravity and stayedness of mind and spirit, not usual in children." This sober estimate of himself indicates, even in his early formative period, a fixity of purpose, a steadiness of will, which would come in good stead when the right purpose should be found and when the will should discover its goal. He was, too, possessed from a very early period of life—from the time he was eleven years old, he says himself—with a passion for purity and righteousness, and he was endowed with a rare sensitiveness of mind for the truth, both in word and deed. "If George says verily there is no altering him," was the comment of those who knew him. It is surely a significant fact that, with all his sensitiveness of spirit, he never appears to have undergone any travail over his own sins, nor to have passed through that experience of conviction of sin which was such a common feature of the evangelical Christianity of his time. From this point of view we may consider him as a good instance of a life conforming to the true normal type—a life unfolding its moral and spiritual powers in harmonious parallelism with the development of its physical and mental powers—for the one ideally normal life which the world has seen was a Life which "increased in wisdom and stature and in favour with God and man." The element of sanity in Fox, the fixity of will and moral purpose, the spiritual earnestness, amounting to an inward passion, the unswerving dedication of himself to the religious life, are surely to be reckoned with by any one who would understand his life, his quest, his discovery, or his mission. It was because he possessed in high degree these rare moral and spiritual traits which are the very core of normality, because in short he was the person he was, that he came upon the *experience* which unified his life, and knew what to do with his discovery when it came to him.

Not only was there an extraordinary heightening of personality and a release of moral and spiritual energy in Fox's own life, as though streams from beyond himself had swept into him, but there was as well a corresponding heightening of life and increase of energy in a large number of those who were reached by his message. His work was almost everywhere attended by moral awakening, by increased intensity of conviction, by the attainment of first-hand experience of Divine reality and a corresponding relaxation of the hold on forms, ceremonies, and dogmas; and, without any apparent effort or pressure, those who were "convinced" took on, as if by natural instinct, the ideas, manners, attitudes, practices, language, and mode of worship which Fox had already adopted. Like the diverse people at Pentecost, they found themselves swept by a common Spirit, and baptized into an integral, organic life. This was largely due to the fact that those who were convinced in the first stages of the movement were already *prepared* for the message which they now heard, and were in an expectant and suggestible state. Not only was the leader developed and his views given direction by the strivings and aspirations of the period, but those who heard his word and believed it, as the message their hearts were seeking, had formed their lives in the same atmosphere, were moved by the same tendencies, and were already feeling vaguely for what they now found. They rose together to a new level, underwent common experiences, and formed a single family group, because they were in the main prepared for the specific way which their leader—the prophet of the period—had discovered as the true line of march.

We must next consider the type of religion which the movement created. Quakerism, as a type of Christianity, is deeply *mystical* and also deeply *prophetical*.

Mysticism is a type of religion as rich and many-sided as life itself—it is, in fact, life itself at its highest inward unity and its most consummate attainment of Reality. The tendency of many who have written about mysticism has been to treat it as one more among the many theoretical "systems" of religious thought, to reduce it to a metaphysic, and to leave the impression on the mind of the reader that it is either the *negative path* which the intellect takes to find God, or an equally empty ecstasy in which the intellect is utterly quiescent. The mystics, however, who have enriched the content and meaning of religion, insist that true mysticism is neither passive nor negative nor theoretical. It is a type of religion, according to them, in which all the deep-lying powers of the personal life come into positive exercise and function, so that there results an experience, not merely emotional, not merely intellectual, not merely volitional, through which the soul finds itself in a love-relation with the Living God. There are all possible stages and degrees of the experience of this "relation" from simple awareness of the soul's Divine Companion to a rapt consciousness of union with the One and Only Reality. The term mystical is properly used for any type of religion which insists upon an immediate inward revelation of God within the sphere of personal experience. The person who has found within the deeps of himself the bubbling streams from the Eternal Fountain of Life, and no longer feels compelled to go back to the pools of tradition or the stagnant wells of authority for his supplies, the person who feels in himself the pulsation of That which Is, and feels as directly sure of God as he is of his own personality, has in so far a mystical religion, though he may have no ecstasies, and may keep a sane and normal hold upon the finite and the visible.[11]

It was through experiences of this first-hand type that the Quaker movement was initiated, and all the primitive leaders of it—"the First Publishers of Truth," as they were called—were recipients of experiences which convinced them that God revealed Himself directly and immediately within themselves. George Fox has given a very simple and impressive account of the experience which ended his long search for somebody who could "speak to his condition" and give him authoritative direction to a religion of verity and reality. "When all my hopes in men," he says, "were gone, so that I had nothing outwardly to help me, nor could I tell what to do, then, O then, I heard a voice which said, There is one, even Christ Jesus that can speak to thy condition; and when I heard it my heart did leap for joy. *I knew experimentally* that Jesus Christ enlightens, gives grace and faith and power. *I now knew God by revelation*, as He who hath the key did open."[12] This is a typical piece of early Quaker biography. The testimony of the Yorkshire yeoman William Dewsbury is not so well known as that of Fox, but it comes up out of actual experience, and it, as well as that of Fox, has the power of a pure and sincere life behind it. His spiritual travail was long and hard, beginning when he was a boy of thirteen. "I heard," he says, "much speaking of God and professing Him in words from the letter of the Scripture, but I met with none that could tell me what God had done for their souls." At length all his "fig-leaf coverings were rent," the Lord "manifested His power" to him, and brought "the immortal seed to birth" within him, and he bears this personal testimony: "I came to my knowledge of eternal life not by the letter of scripture, nor from hearing men speak of God, but by the Inspiration of the Spirit of Jesus Christ who is worthy to open the seals."[13]

The call of James Nayler is a striking instance of this type of *experience*. "I was," he says, "at the plough, meditating on the things of God, and suddenly I heard a Voice saying unto me, 'Get thee out from thy kindred and from thy father's house.' I did exceedingly rejoice that I had heard the Voice of that God which I had professed from a child, but had never known." He was interrupted as he was telling his narrative in Court, and asked if he *heard* the Voice. "Yes," says Nayler, "I did *hear* it."[14] Francis Howgill, who was one of the rare and beautiful spirits of the movement, has given us a very fresh account of the type of experience which made life new for these men. "The Kingdom of Heaven," he says, "did gather us and catch us all as in a net . . . and the Lord appeared daily to us, to our astonishment, amazement, and great admiration insomuch that we often said one unto another, with great joy of heart, 'What? Is the Kingdom of God come to be with men?' "[15]

One after another, in their quaint phraseology, the creative leaders of the movement declare that they have "felt the bubblings of the everlasting springs of Life," or that they have "felt the healings drop into their souls from under God's wings," or that they have been "begotten of the Eternal Word and born of the Immortal Seed," or that "God has opened the Springs of the Great Deep and overflowed their hearts, and they have seen and felt beyond demonstration and speech." Early Quaker literature abounds, too, with illustrations of the fact that these "First Publishers" had not only partaken of extraordinary inward experiences themselves, but were also possessed of very unusual power over others. George Canby's account of his "convincement" through the instrumentality of William Dewsbury is a good specimen case: "The power of God was mightily upon William and fixing his Eyes upon me, [he] Declared what the Lord putt into his mouth to me in particular and I did truly Witness the Word of the Lord to be Quick and Powerfull which cut me to the heart, that I fell Down in the House ffloor as Dead to all Appearance as any Clogg or Stone. When I came to sence again, he had got me up in his Armes; so that I can truly say I was smitten down to the Ground by the Liveing Power of the Lord as sure as ever Saul was in his way to Damascus." [16] An officer in Cromwell's army who heard James Nayler preach after he had had his experience, but before he became a Quaker, was aware of such "power and reaching energy" that he felt struck with more terror by the searching power of the preaching than by the battle of Dunbar!

It is a matter of little importance what name is given to this type of religion.

> A learned man
> Could give it a clumsy name.

The important fact is obvious enough, that here in the English Commonwealth there now appeared a group of persons— plain, simple persons without technical learning—who succeeded in passing from knowledge about God, knowledge which consisted of demonstration from scripture texts, "notional knowledge" they aptly called it, to an inward, first-hand experience which was so vivid, so warm and intimate, so mightily transforming, that they one and all were convinced that they had found God in the present tense. In the earliest stage of the movement there was no attempt to formulate the experience, to reduce it to a doctrine; they felt it, lived in it, transmitted it, and believed that it was soon to be a universal fact of personal life—a Pentecost for all humanity.

There can be no question that the experience which came to these men—the experience of finding God, it seemed to them—was extraordinarily dynamic. Whatever a searching psychology may say about it as a method of arriving at extra-human knowledge, the experience was attended by *a great release of energy, and the formation of vastly enhanced personality.* Men, formerly somewhat below the normal in physical stamina, became capable of tasks quite beyond the ordinary limits of physical effort, and were able to endure a regime of organized and unorganized persecution which almost passes the belief of this age of undisturbed toleration. But more striking than this heightened power of endurance was the heightened power of mind and spirit which the movement reveals. Persons who had occupied only the most humble stations in life, unschooled in books and unpractised in affairs, by some sudden alchemy became the exponents of a new message and conception of life, the powerful and convincing preachers of a fresh word of truth, the champions of new moral and social ideals, and the organizers of a unique Christian Society. The mark of their little learning is no doubt upon all their work, and in the long run had disastrous consequences, but the *élan* and marching power of the movement is everywhere evident in the chapters of this history, and the primary source of this heightened energy was this mystical experience—this consciousness that God was inwardly revealed.

But there was another strand of influence to be reckoned with, which for want of a better name I shall call *prophetism.* These leaders believed that the Spirit of God was poured out upon them, as of old it had been; that they were called to be the *prophets* to their age, and that the language of Old and New Testament prophecy and apocalypse was actually fulfilled in their experiences.

I do not raise the question whether they actually foresaw and foretold events or not, for prophecy in its true meaning and significance has nothing to do with magical foretelling. The prophet is a person who is profoundly conscious that he is a divinely selected herald, that he speaks *for* God, and is under commission to utter the will and purpose of God to his age. From time immemorial the persons who have felt this exalted commission and have spoken under this high conviction have made free use of the glowing language of their predecessors, and have employed the common stock of ideas and enthusiasms preserved in the creative literature of prophecy and revelation. The public ministry and the biographies of the early Quakers are saturated with this strain. Their testimonies are breathlessly daring, but there can, I think, be little doubt that they sincerely believed that they had a right to apply the most exalted scripture language to their own inward events, and there can be as little doubt that this prophetical and apocalyptic element vastly helped to produce the mental and emotional climate and atmosphere of the movement, and added much to the warmth and fervour and conquering power of it. "I had," says Fox in his account of his spiritual travail, "great openings concerning the things written in the Revelations, and when I spake of them the priests and professors would say *That* was a sealed book and would have kept me out of it. But I told them Christ could open the seals and that they [the things written in Revelation] were the nearest things to us, for the epistles were written to the saints that lived in former ages, but the Revelations were written of things to come."[17] Again he says: "I heard a voice which did say, Thou serpent! thou dost seek to destroy the life, but canst not; for the sword which keepeth the Tree of Life shall destroy thee, . . . my inward mind being joined to His [Christ's] good Seed, that bruised the head of this serpent."[18] "A pure fire appeared in me; then I saw how He [Christ] sat as a refiner's fire and as the fuller's soap."[19] "And I saw the mountains burning up, and the rubbish and the rough and crooked ways and places made smooth and plain, that the Lord might come into His tabernacle. These things are to be found in man's heart."[20] Finally comes the great testimony: "Now was I come up in Spirit through the Flaming Sword, into the paradise of God. All things were new; and all the creation gave another smell!"[21] Fox's prophetical conviction comes out in its full significance in the contrast which he draws between the experience of the traditional minister and his own experience. "Have any of you," he asks, "ever had the word of the Lord to speak to a definite people? Have any of you ever had a command or word immediately from the Lord, or do you speak of other men's experiences? To receive and go with a message, and to have a word from the Lord, as the prophets and apostles did, *and as I have done*, is quite another thing."[22]

The *Journal* abounds in passages in which the glowing oriental imagery of the prophets and the transcendent pomp of their language are used to describe what is transpiring in the kingdom of his own soul or to portray the contemporary spiritual events of his time. Not only did Fox use this glowing language and imagery for inward events, but all his followers did the same with even less restraint. Here is a good specimen of the type from the pen of Thomas Camm of Westmorland, who in the most simple and naïve fashion describes the mission of the man who had brought such a new day to that country: "That ffaithfull and honorable servant of ye Lord, G. ff. whome God Almighty in his tender years visited with ye day spring from on high, in ye Revellation of his son Jesus Christ . . . became A Child thereof, qualified to turne people from darkness to light and from Satan's power to Christ the Savior and great power of God. Him the great God sanctified by his eternall word and made him [a] Messinger and Minister to bring Glad tideings to ye poore, and delivrance to ye Captive Soulls to proclaime a Jubille and delivrance to ye prisoners of hope."[23]

William Dewsbury's work in Yorkshire is told in this vivid manner: "His Testimony was Peirceing and very powerfull, so as the Earth Shoke before him, The Mountains did melt at the power of the Lord, which exceedingly in a Wonderfull manner broke forth in these Dayes in our holy Assemblies to the Renting of many hearts. Oh! It was a Glorious Day, in which the Lord Wonderfully appeared for the bringing down the Lofty and high minded, and Exalting that of Low degree.

Many faces did gather Paleness, and the Stout hearted were made to Bow and strong Oakes to bend before the Lord."[24]

Richard Hubberthorne, in the early glow of his new-found life, writes to Fox of how his "blind eyes are opened," though "the bond woman and her son" are not yet utterly cast out; but he concluded: "Pray that I may be keeped not to boast above my measure, but may walk in the easy and gentle leadings of the Lamb, and may drink of those rivers in which thou swims."[25]

Margaret Fell, who at times pushed apocalyptic language to the edge of danger, furnishes many good illustrations of this typical prophetism. Writing in 1653 to Colonel West, a member of the Nominated Parliament, she says: "Do what the Lord moves thee, and what He makes way for thee: For it is no Man's strength nor power that we look at, but the Lord alone; who is the same to us that He was to Daniel in the Lion's Den and the Three Children in the Fiery Furnace"; and to her friends she says: "Dear hearts, this is the Day of your Visitation and Salvation, for the Everlasting God, which is the Life, Light and Substance of Life is risen and arising, and raising up the Dead to hear the Voice of the Son of God, and they that hear do live. And the dead Bones is coming together and standing up; yea, the Earth is giving up her Dead, if you be faithful to the measure of God's Spirit."[26]

Thus the prophets in all ages have felt and have spoken. The outward is husk and shell; from within comes the Resurrection and the Life, recreating the world and making all things new. St. Francis of Assisi and his Calabrian predecessor Joachim of Floris are striking illustrations of the power which may attend a genuine revival of prophetism; and Savonarola is a memorable example of the way in which a creative leader can draw upon the language of prophecy and apocalypse to revivify his own age, and can make spiritual and moral realities vivid and coercive enough to call men from flesh-pots and commerce and pleasure-aims to a real preparation of the soul for its eternal destiny.

But while emphasizing these two predominant aspects of

the early Quaker movement, we must not overlook or underestimate its moral and social features. Prophetism is often dreamy, visionary, and seething with ill-directed enthusiasm. Mysticism is frequently self-centred and absorbed with the inward gaze.

> Was I too dark a prophet when I said
> To those who went upon the Holy Quest,
> That most of them would follow wandering fires,
> Lost in the quagmire? . . .
> And out of those to whom the vision came
> My greatest hardly will believe he saw;
> Another hath beheld it afar off,
> *And leaving human wrongs to right themselves,*
> *Cares but to pass into the silent life.*[27]

There was, however, in the Quaker movement a moral earnestness and a social intensity which saved it from the easy pitfalls of mystical quests. If these men had their moments of transport when they felt themselves "in the Paradise of God" and perceived that "the whole creation had a new smell," they never lost their hold upon the central purpose of their lives—to transform this present world and these actual human fellows about them to the end that the will of God might become the will of men, and that society here on earth might take on a likeness to the Kingdom of Heaven. Fox has his first *awakening* in his nineteenth year, not over his own sins, but over the moral conditions and social customs about him.[28] "I could not sleep," he says, "but walked up and down, and prayed and cried to the Lord." He was not striving after exalted states of mind; he seems never concerned about his own soul. The travail of spirit which "made him lean for years" was for the moral and spiritual deliverance of the heavy-laden people whom he saw. His vigorous prayer frequently uttered is that "the seed of God might be atop of the Devil and all his works," and that "the Seed might reign." "The burden of the mystery" of evil in its many concrete forms was always upon his spirit; the "heavy and weary

weight" of human wrongs in the world around him always
oppressed him. His emphasis is always on the practical and
pragmatic bearing of his doctrine of a Light within: "Mind
that of God within you. Stand for the good of your people.
Take off all oppression; and set up justice over all."[29] The peculiar "testimonies" which played such a striking role in the
early period of Quakerism had their origin and ground in the
deep-seated purpose to break down the slavery of superficial
fashions and cramping customs, and to restore individual responsibility, spiritual initiative, and personal autonomy. Man
himself, with his inherent divine rights and his eternal destiny,
is put in the place of sacred and time-honoured *systems*. Whatever hampers, limits, restrains, spoils human powers is to go
down at all costs in life and suffering, and whatever enlarges,
liberates, and lifts man has a place in the programme of these
"Children of the Light." It was in this focussing upon moral
effort that the Quakers differed most from the other sects of the
Commonwealth period. Their "views" were not novel or
original. Every one of their peculiar ideas had already been
proclaimed by some individual or by some religious party.
What was *new* was the fusing of their ideas into one living
truth, which was henceforth to be done, was to be put into
life and made to march. They fully shared the practical spirit
of their interesting contemporary Gerrard Winstanley, who
finely says: "My mind was not at rest because nothing was
acted; and thoughts ran in me that words and writings were
all nothing and must die; for action is the life of all, and if
thou dost not act thou dost nothing."[30]

So absorbed in work for human betterment were they, so
consecrated to the task of remaking the world, that many who
have studied the early Quakers have seen only this practical
—or perhaps ideal—aspect of the movement, and have neglected the mystical feature of their religion. But both these
aspects belong together as much as the concave and convex
sides of a circle do. Mere social propaganda and bare philan-
thropic activity untouched by a vision of the penetrating, co-
operating presence of God as the resident power of all per-

manent advance are thin and weak, and all mystical insights which end in emotional thrills, vapouring enthusiasms, and states of moveless ecstasy are blind and futile. This Quaker movement is significant, is worth studying, because it shows both strands woven into one organic whole. There are marks of weakness and imperfection apparent in it. It has, as all earthly movements have, its obvious limitations and its petty traits, but it is nevertheless a very real *experiment in religion*, and one that is full of lessons for our age and for all Christian communions.

NOTES

1. *Spiritual Reformers in the 16th and 17th Centuries*, 1914.
2. Fox calls these Nottinghamshire people "shattered Baptists," because they broke up into small groups, with characteristically different tendencies. Some of them seem to have lost their moral earnestness and seriousness of aim, and others, remaining still intensely religious, declined to affiliate with any organized Christian body.
3. *Journal* (bi-cent. edn.), i. 6.
4. *Ibid.* i. 20.
5. *Ibid.* i. 444.
6. *Ibid.* i. 453.
7. *Ibid.* ii. pp. 132–139.
8. *Ibid.* i. pp. 77–78.
9. A man in Carlisle in 1653 could not bear "the power of his eyes," but cried out, "Do not pierce me so with thy eyes; keep thy eyes off me."—*Journal*, i. p. 167.
10. *Journal*, i. p. 133.
11. The special form which such experiences take depends largely upon the peculiar type of psychical constitution which the person possesses.
12. Condensed from the *Journal*, i. 11–12.
13. William Dewsbury, "The New Birth," *Works*, pp. 44–57.
14. *Works*, p. 12.
15. Howgill's Testimony to Burrough, printed in the Introduction to Burrough's *Works*.
16. *First Publishers of Truth* (ed. by N. Penney, 1909) p. 290.
17. *Journal*, i. 8.
18. *Ibid.* i. 13.
19. *Ibid.* i. 15.
20. *Ibid.* i. 16.
21. *Ibid.* i. 28.
22. *Journal*, i. pp. 126–127, not *verbatim*.
23. *First Publishers of Truth*, pp. 241–242.
24. *Ibid.* p. 294.

25. Hubberthorne to Fox, *Swarthm. Colln.* iv. 4.
26. Margaret Fox, *Works*, pp. 43 and 48.
27. Tennyson, *The Holy Grail*.
28. See *Journal*, i. p. 3.
29. Fox's Letter to the Governor of Rhode Island (1672).
30. *A Watchword to the City of London.*

4

The Second Period of Quakerism

In *The Beginnings of Quakerism* we were dealing at every point with a "movement." It was creative, enthusiastic, and full of surprises. In this volume Quakerism is still a movement, but it is plainly in the stage of organization, consolidation, and congealment. When the creative leaders of the great period pass off the scene, as they do toward the end of this volume, we find that the movement is pretty well stiffened and arrested, and that a system is emerging. We are passing from dynamic to static Quakerism. So long as the world continued hostile to it, and endeavoured to suppress it or transform it, it revealed an amazing vitality and energy of endurance. The men and women who shaped the Quaker history of the creative stage were sublimely indifferent to consequences. They were possessed of a vision and dedicated to a mission which made everything else on earth secondary and more or less unimportant. That situation makes an heroic story, but the very success of the policy of uncomprising endurance makes the later epochs of Quakerism less heroic and less interesting. The work of forcing back the sea and building the dykes makes necessarily a different type of persons from those who are "born to peace in the lee of the dykes." All movements of every sort undergo some such change of type.

It would seem appropriate that this Introduction should deal in the main with the transforming effect of consolidation and organization, since this is the peculiar aspect which forms the connecting link between the preceding volume and the succeeding volumes of this series.[1]

My preliminary researches, in *Studies in Mystical Religion* and in *Spiritual Reformers of the Sixteenth and Seventeenth Centuries*, have conclusively shown that there was a long historical

preparation for the Quaker movement, and that it was a legitimate outcome of this painful travail of lonely souls and per-
secuted groups who were striving for an adequate spiritual
reformation of the Church. One of the most remarkable
features of this historical preparation was the almost complete
absence of organization throughout the entire period. The
movement went steadily forward by the propagation and
transmission of ideas, by personal inspiration and by what, for
want of a better term, we call contagion of ideals. Nobody
during this time appeared with a genius for organization. In
fact, the aspirations of the spirit of the movement were positively unfriendly to organization. As is the case with all
movements which are at heart profoundly mystical, the
leaders of this movement were afraid of the hampering, con-
tracting effects of method and system, and, as a consequence,
it maintained its fluidity for more than a hundred years without ever losing its power of propagation or its contagious
growth.

The Church which the spiritual reformers aimed to create
was an invisible Church, rather than a visible, organized, and
empirical one. They took the early unorganized stage of
apostolic Christianity as their model. They no doubt somewhat
idealized and glorified this apostolic Church of saints, but so,
too, did all types of reformers idealize the primitive Church
and set it in sharp contrast to the Church with which they
were familiar. Luther himself, in his early reforming period,
conceived of the true Church as a spiritual congregation, composed only of the new-born, transformed persons, possessed of
faith and insight, and all together ministering to the spiritual
life of all. "I believe," he wrote, "that there is on earth, wide
as the world is, only one holy universal Christian Church,
which is nothing else than the community [*Gemeinde*] of the
saints."[2] This conception always remained as the ideal of the
spiritual reformers. The mediaeval Church, with its creeds,
its hierarchy, its magical sacraments, its compromises with
the world, its external imperial authority, its ambitions, its
corruptions, its multitude of nominal or titular members,

seemed to these high-minded idealists "an apostate Church," incapable of being reformed. It was to them a work of misguided "Babel-builders." They utterly disapproved of the course which they saw the great reformers, Luther, Zwingli and Calvin, taking to correct and remedy the intolerable situation. The alliance with the State, which was a feature of all reformed Churches, seemed to them an unholy alliance. The survivals of untransformed theology, the preservation of ancient superstitions, the continuance in the new Churches of unspiritual, nominal members, the exaltation of the letter of Scripture, and the use of persecution as a method of forcing uniformity appeared to them to be regrettable relics of paganism and apostasy. They would have none of it.

They were determined to create, or rather to restore, a wholly different type of Church. It was to have no connection whatever with the State. It was to have no infallible creed. It was to be governed by no authoritative hierarchy. It was to have no *essential* forms, rites, ritual, or ceremonies. It was not even to be an "organization" in the strict sense of the word. It was to be a fellowship, a society, a communion. All persons in all lands and in all ages who have been born of God, who partake of Christ's spirit, who are united in the bonds of love, who are travailing for the Kingdom of God, who experience the communion of the Holy Spirit, belong to this Church. It is thus both visible and invisible. It is on the earth but at the same time a super-temporal communion. It is the bride of Christ, the organ of the Spirit, the entire congregation and assembly of the saints. It is tied and bound to no fixed and unchanging external system or order. It is the growing, expanding revelation of God through men, and its one essential mark is *life*, but always life revealing itself through love and sacrifice and service. As Sebastian Franck (1499–1542) enthusiastically declares: "It is neither prince nor peasant, food nor drink, hat nor coat, here nor there, yesterday nor to-morrow, baptism nor circumcision, nor anything whatever that is external, but peace and joy in the Holy Spirit, unalloyed love out of a pure heart and good conscience, and an unfeigned faith."[3] These men, though trained in the universities of their time, were childlike in their naïve simplicity. They assumed that religion as a living, inward experience would take care of itself in the world. It would need no external supports nor contrivances. Christ, the eternal Word, the Spirit of Truth, the Light shining immediately in the human soul, would guard, guide, protect, create, construct His own Church, if only men would let Him work unhindered. Once more as in the creative apostolic days, the Spirit would fall upon the obedient, responsive, faithful believers, endow them with gifts, endue them with power, and through them continue His revelation of Light, Life, Love, and Truth. Their Church was thus to be spontaneous, free, vital, expanding, joyous, and potentially universal, because it was to be the one body of Christ.

There can be, I think, no question that George Fox began his mission with that ideal in mind. He became convinced that all existing Churches were in "apostasy." The preface to his *Great Mistery* (1658), though actually written by Edward Burrough, clearly expresses Fox's mind and position. This remarkable document says: "As our hearts inclined to the light which shined in every one of us we came to know the perfect estate of the Church; her estate before the apostles' days, and in the apostles' days, and since the days of the apostles. Her present state we found to be as a woman who had once been clothed with the sun and the moon under her feet, who had brought forth him that was to rule the nations; but she had fled into the wilderness and was there sitting desolate!" Again it says: "As for all Churches (so called) and professions and gatherings of people, we beheld you all in the apostasy and degeneration from the true Church, not being gathered by the Spirit of the Lord, nor anointed thereby, as the true members of Christ ever were, but to be in a form, and in forms of righteousness without the power, and in imitations without life and perfect knowledge." This preface boldly declares that no true reformation has yet taken place, and that the existing Churches lack a true worship, a real religion, and practices that have life and power.

George Fox and his early followers believed that they were called to carry out the true reformation, to restore apostolic Christianity, and to make a fresh beginning in England of the Church of Christ. They never thought of themselves as a "sect," or as one "Church" among many Protestant "Churches." They thought of themselves as forming a group, a fellowship, a society they called it, of persons who were a living part of this true Church of the ages. All saints who have ever lived and who have shaped their spiritual lives by the light of Christ were members with them and with them constituted the true "Seed of God," the one Church, with Christ as its Head and Life. They believed that this Church was as wide as the world, and they went forth with unbounded faith and enthusiasm to discover in all lands those who were true fellow-members with them in this great household of God, and who were the hidden Seed of God. It was not to be a man-made or a man-governed institution. It was to be a Christ-made and a Christ-governed society or body. It was in conception a living organism rather than an organization. It was in ideal to be the work and creation of the Spirit of Christ, operating from within: and not the work and creation of human hands, building from the outside. In theory the Society of Friends had no visible head. Nobody managed it, nobody directed it. Every step was taken, however momentous, however trivial, by the entire group acting, as it believed, under the direction and guidance of the Spirit. All ministry was, in ideal, Divinely initiated and given through unordained persons who had listened and heard and who spoke because the word of God had come to them. All the work of propagation, the efforts to reach and gather the hidden Seed of God, were undertaken by men and women who were "called" out and qualified for this Divine business.

It is a mark of the wisdom and sanity of George Fox that, mystic and idealist as he was, he faced the facts of life, he learnt from experience, he came to see that disembodied spiritual movements cannot succeed and do a permanent work

in the world; and, when the hour came for it, he took the
leadership in organizing the Society of Friends for its abiding,
expanding mission. This was obviously a delicate and difficult undertaking. It was in some degree a surrender of the
original ideal, perhaps we had better say of the primitive
dream. John Wilkinson and John Story, the leaders of the
opposition to the organizing work of Fox, were endeavouring
to stand uncompromisingly for the "pure" primitive ideal.
They were the champions of an abstract liberty, theorists who
refused utterly to regard consequences or to take account of
things as they are. They defied experience. Fox, on the other
hand, yielded to the pressure of unescapable facts. He had
been a keen observer of events and tendencies within the fellowship of which he was the leading spirit. He noted the
disintegrating forces. He saw the necessity for co-operation,
even though it might involve some surrender of individual
privilege. He was willing to adjust to the conditions and requirements of social or group existence, though it meant a
reduction of his early ideals. There was no way of going forward at all without some compromise of abstract theory.
Usually "stiff as a tree," in the words of his Scarborough
jailers, he bent in this crisis and thus gave his movement the
possibility of a successful future. Deep-seated troubles and
hampering limitations lay concealed in the system of organization that was gradually worked out for the growing Society,
but *any* type of organization that might have been adopted
would have brought its peculiar difficulties and its limitations
to this enthusiastic, spiritual undertaking. To organize is to
come under the sway of habit and custom. It more or less locks
up a movement and turns it into a system. Initiative decreases.
Plural possibilities are eliminated. Enthusiasm wanes. A
cooling process succeeds. Conservatism and loyalty to the
status quo become powerful forces. The very things which
make life possible entail at the same time perils and dangers.

It must be said, however, that the primitive form of organization which was gradually worked out by George Fox
and his helpers for the Society of Friends was admirably fitted

to the genius of the movement. They gave as much scope as was possible under any system for the free, unhindered circulation of the Spirit. They got as far away as possible from the model of the state Church, the Church as conceived and constructed by the great Protestant reformers. They kept close to the ideal of a fellowship of believers, living in obedience to the Spirit revealed within them. Their Society was in idea a complete democracy, that is to say no imposed official or head was ever to interfere with any member's individual liberty. And yet it was to be a democracy of a new type. The individuals composing the Society were no longer to be thought of as bare, isolated, self-seeking units, acting capriciously. Each member of the Society was, in their thought, an over-individual. He was to be a partaker of the life of the Spirit; he was to be an organ of the in-dwelling Christ; he was inwardly to be raised into new and corporate life with all the other members. It was thus in thought and purpose a Divine democracy, a real communion of saints, living here below but sharing the life and mind of the eternal, invisible Christ. It was in essence a miniature kingdom of God, a little visible part of the whole family of God, a tiny fragment of the invisible Church. It had no constitution, no creed, no sacraments, no clergy, no ordained officials, no infallibilities, except the infallibility of the guiding Spirit. With all its limitations, this Society, organized in the Restoration period, against the protests of the pure idealists, has proved to be the most impressive experiment in Christian history of a group-mysticism, a religious body practising corporate silence as the basis of worship and maintaining a fundamental faith in Spirit-guided ministry.

The formulation of Quaker doctrine was, in my judgment, not as happy, was not performed in a manner as accordant with the genius of the movement as was the form of the organization of the Society. The main difficulty with the formulation of doctrine in general is that it must always of necessity be done in terms of the prevailing metaphysics of the period. It is an obvious fact that systems of metaphysics are

doomed to become out-dated and inadequate with the process
of thought. Fashions in metaphysics are notoriously subject
to change. The result is that the religious truth of a movement, once locked up and encased in a system of thought
which dies and gets left behind, is itself in danger of crystallization and arrest. Just this common course of events has occurred with the formal declaration of the Quaker principle.
In the first stage Quakerism remained experimental, vital, un-
formulated. George Fox was naïve, spontaneous, and unreflective. He knew no school metaphysics. He simply called
men to "that of God in themselves." He took almost exactly
the position of the spiritual reformers. He assumed that universal experience bore witness to a Divine light within man.
He rested his entire faith upon the native testimony of the
soul. Wherever man is found some moral and spiritual truths
are revealed in him. How the Divine and human can be conjunct, how God and man can correspond and co-operate, did
not greatly concern him. He was satisfied with the clear fact.
He was ready to trust the soul. But in a world of endless debate
and conflict, the problem of the Divine-human relationship
was sure to arise and become urgent. Controversy was inevitable; it was the very air men breathed in this seventeenth
century. There could be no continuous propaganda of the faith
without a definite exposition and defence of it. That meant
that sooner or later it must get into the common theological
terminology of the time.

This work of translating the Quaker faith into a contemporary system of thought was performed by Robert Barclay of
Scotland. He was a highly endowed person, of rare natural
gifts. He was broadly educated and carefully trained as a
scholar. He was typically Scotch in his bent and fondness for
exact logical comprehension. He bears his frequent testimony
as a convinced Quaker that experience is everything and system almost nothing, and yet, in spite of that personal testimony, he goes insistently forward with the development of
his elaborate logically-linked system as though—however his
heart felt—his mind believed that truth could not maintain

itself and prevail without the solid armour of logic. He was above everything else a good man, pure, high-minded, noble, dedicated. He does not understand the common people by native instinct as George Fox does. His blood and nurture separate him from the rank and file, without his intention of having it so. He is most at home and at his best when he is talking with Princess Elizabeth or writing to her. This Stuart princess was one of the most learned women in Europe, the intimate friend and correspondent of Descartes, a combination of philosopher and saint and, in her later life, almost persuaded to become a Friend.

Barclay possessed a beautiful inner spirit. His character was one peculiarly marked by sweetness, though at the same time not lacking in firmness and strength. His religion went all through him. His soul was reached by a real experience, and all the springs of his life were fed by his experimental discovery of God. With noble purpose and with the loftiest intentions he undertook the difficult task of expounding the truth of the Inward Light, as a universal religion.

The *Apology for the True Christian Divinity, as the same is held forth and preached by the People called in scorn Quakers*, was written when Barclay was twenty-seven and is an extraordinary book. The range of Barclay's knowledge of Scripture and of the Fathers and Reformers of the Church, and the depth of his penetration, compare favourably with the same qualities in the first edition of Calvin's *Institutes*, written when Calvin was twenty-six. A primary difficulty with the *Apology*, however, lies in the fact that the writer of it belonged to a fundamentally different school of thought from that in which the leaders of Quakerism moved. These early Quaker founders had broken away completely from the theological doctrines which the Protestant Reformers inherited and re-formulated. They cut straight across and left on one side the whole loop of theological "notions." They proposed to leave the old behind and to make a new beginning. The theological concepts about which men preached and debated seemed to them hollow, empty, and dead. They were as opposed to restoring

these outworn "notions" as they were to reviving the superstitions of the mediaeval Church. "The dead might bury the
dead;" their business was proclaiming a gospel of Life and
Light. They plainly meant to keep religion in the warm and
living currents of experience; to have their message and their
entire proclamation spring out of realities discovered within
the purview of their own souls. The Calvinistic account of
God and man and salvation was to them an unnecessary ap-
pendix to the eternal, living Word of God; an unwarranted
supplement to apostolic Christianity. They lived and thought
in another world of ideas, they were the inheritors of the
long labours of mystics, heretics, martyrs, and spiritual
prophets, and it was their peculiar mission to transmit this
type of inner religion, at length freed from the encasing bonds
of man-made doctrines.

Barclay, on the contrary, decides to find out how Quakerism
stands with Reformation doctrines, and to adjust the new as
far as possible with the old. He reveals at every point an
intimate and minute acquaintance with the entire history of
theological doctrine. He knows, as I have said, the writings
of the Fathers, the Schoolmen, and the Reformers. What he
does not know, at least not intimately or profoundly, is the
line of spiritual predecessors who have prepared the way in the
wilderness for Quakerism. He had never travelled over this
highway. He had missed the little books which came out of
the deep experience of the great mystics. He was not familiar
with the spiritual contemporaries of Luther and Calvin and
Arminius, who essayed to mark out a new path to the Kingdom. He had not read, and one can but wish he had done so,
the fresh and liberating interpretations of Christianity given
by the Cambridge Platonists, Benjamin Whichcote, John
Smith, and their friends. Here was a way of thought kindred
to the spirit and genius of the Quaker principle and ideals.
But Barclay's intellectual world attached elsewhere. He undertook not to reinterpret the Quaker principle in terms of this
wider, fresher, deeper movement of thought, but rather to
challenge the prevailing Protestant system of thought, and to

show how this system would look when adjusted to fit the principle of the Inward Light. That course, judged histori- cally, seems to me a pity. It was done with real genius, but a wholly different type of interpretation would have been far better for the "truth." It was unfortunate to lock up this new idea in that old system.

We find ourselves in the *Apology* back again with the ancient conception of "man," so familiar in the theories of the dog- matic theologians. Friends had begun their movement with a bold challenge to this Augustinian dogma. Fox, speaking out of his own experience, says that he had gravity and stayedness of mind as a child; he was from his earliest days kept pure, and when he was eleven years old he knew pureness and righteousness.[4] His experience of God in his own soul en- abled him to take a fundamental view of man very unlike that of the speculative theologians. He trusts experience for his theory of man and passes by on the other side and leaves be- hind the dogma about man, as his spiritual predecessors had also done. The mysticism of George Fox is characteristically affirmative. He testifies elsewhere to a first-hand consciousness of God. He knows of nothing to prevent God and man finding one another and enjoying one another. Death and darkness abound, but God still more abounds and is "over" them. There is a busy Satan at work in the world, but God is "atop" of him, and "the Seed of God" is a reigning, victorious thing. Fox emphatically belongs in the anti-Augustinian movement. Barclay, however, goes back to the accepted dogma about man, and adopts it as his basis, and then endeavours to alter it to fit his view of the Inward Light. "Man by nature, man as he is *man*," Barclay says, "is corrupt and fallen." "No real good proceedeth from his nature as he is man." "A seed of sin is transmitted to all men from Adam"; "a seed is propa- gated to all men which in its own nature is sinful and inclines men to inquity." No good, he declares, should be ascribed to the natural man; he is "polluted in all his ways"; he is "void of righteousness and of the knowledge of God"; he is "out of the way and in short unprofitable"; he is "unfit to make one step toward heaven."[5] A good illustration of Barclay's argumentative method is found in his comment upon the text Genesis viii. 21, "The imagination of man's heart is evil from his youth." "From which," he proceeds, "I thus argue:

"If the thoughts of man's heart be not only evil, but always evil; then are they, as they simply proceed from his heart, neither good in part nor at any time.

" But the first is true; therefore the last.

"Again,

"If man's thoughts be always and only evil, then are they altogether useless and ineffectual to him in the things of God.

" But the first is true, therefore the last."[6]

This proposition regarding the dogma of man's sinful nature is established, after the usual manner of dogmatic theologians, by a judicious selection of Scripture texts, treated in a similar way to that employed by Calvin to prove his theories of "man." The Adamic story is taken as factual history; the theory of the transmission of "a seed of sin" as taught by Calvin is accepted as though it were an essential part of the gospel.[7] No attempt is made to sound the deeps of human experience itself. It does not occur to him that this is a question to be settled by the testimony of the soul, and that first of all one ought to investigate actual human life as it is and to build the theory on facts of experience. He piles up instead a structure of texts and considers that the far-reaching conclusion has been proved.

Barclay means by "the natural man" man as he would be if he were stripped of all altruistic traits, of all spiritual potency, of every upward-striving tendency, a being who is a bundle of selfish instincts and passions. He is, for theological purposes, reduced to his lowest terms. "He differeth," Barclay says, "as he is mere man, no otherwise from beasts than by the rational property," and it quickly appears that "the rational property" is nothing but a logical faculty, a cognitive capacity to form conceptions about the external world and to argue from them to other conceptions equally external. There is nothing in this "natural man" that can in any degree appreciate or apprehend spiritual truth. In his own nature he can discern nothing of the things of God; he can do no good thing; he is utterly carnal and a continual prey to evil propensities. It needs hardly to be said at this date that there is no such being as this so-called "natural man." He is an artificial construction. He is no more real than the Jabberwock is. He is an abstract figure, existing nowhere outside of books. Real man in his native fundamental being is both altruistic and selfish, both sympathetic and egotistic. It is as "natural" for him to love others as it is to promote self-interest. It is as instinctive to be social as it is to be individualistic. Man as man carries in the very ground of his nature a self-transcending spirit. Something from beyond his finite limits is bound up in him and for ever pushes him out of himself and draws him on. Every revelation of the real nature of God that has come to us has come through man. Man's spirit is a candle of the Lord and can burn with a revealing flame. God and man for ever belong together, and only by an arid and artificial metaphysics are they so sundered that man is reduced to this poor thing called "mere man." "The truths of God are connatural to the soul of man," Benjamin Whichcote was saying in the very period when Barclay was writing his *Apology*, "and the soul of man makes no more resistance to them than the air does to light."[8]

It is peculiarly tragic that the fresh discovery of spiritual truth which Friends made should so quickly have been attached to the ancient dogmatic theory of "man," because it is a sound principle that "there can be no true doctrine of God that is not based on a true doctrine of man."[9] If man is not, in his real nature, a being through whom God can reveal Himself, then our world is doomed to be a godless world, for there is no other way for revelation to come. As soon as we turn to experience, however, we are at once reassured. Man, with all his faults and failures, with all his blunders and sins, is a being who lives by ideals which come from beyond himself, who organizes all the facts of his experience under universal forms of thought that ally him at once with a deeper universe of spiritual realities. He is always living for values and by visions that raise him out of the category of "mere man." Something not of matter nor of space and time, something drawn from a realm of Spirit, is woven into the very structure of his soul and makes him akin to God whether he chooses to be the conscious child of God or not. The presence of the eternal reality, that gives permanence to any of our facts of experience, is indissolubly joined to our consciousness of self. We never possess the whole of ourselves. We are organic with a wider inner life than we have yet consciously made our own. The margins of our souls stretch farther than we dream.

And though thy soul sail leagues and leagues beyond,
Still leagues beyond those leagues, there is more sea.[10]

It is possible, no doubt, to draw a narrow boundary around an abstract self and call the poor thing "mere man," and then to demonstrate that of itself it has no spiritual powers—only in every case it is man himself who makes this mere-man creation. It is not one of God's real men!

When once this fatal reduction or truncation of man has been made, the theologian must of necessity have recourse to miracle to make such a being spiritual. Salvation can then, of course, be effected only by some form of supernatural mediation. Here one discovers the peculiar ingenuity of the particular theologian. Some *vehiculum Dei*—*i.e.* mechanism by which the remote God is miraculously brought into operation in the otherwise unspiritual soul—must be contrived. Barclay's ingenuity is here of a high order. He admits "the miserable and depraved condition" of mere man,[11] but he is confident that there is an adequate supernatural provision to meet this *impasse*. Christ by His death "purchased for man" a universal Light or Divine Seed. "Through the merits of this death" this Divine Light is conferred upon every person born into the world, and "puts all mankind into a capacity for salvation."[12] "The Lord hath been pleased," Barclay says, "to reserve the more full discovery of this glorious and evangelical dispensation to this our own age."[13] In other words, he believes that the great discovery which "the Children of the Light" have made is this provision of salvation by means of a work of Divine grace within the heart of man. It was, according to his exposition, just this *gift* of light and grace which Christ "purchased" for man on the Cross of Calvary. Only it seems passing strange that there was any necessity to "purchase" at such a price a grace which one would suppose would have spontaneously flowed out from the heart of a loving Father-God.

This Light, bestowed on man, as we have seen, through the purchase of Christ's death, does not in any sense belong to man's own nature, for "the natural man is wholly excluded from having any place or portion in his own salvation, by any acting, moving, or working of his own."[14] This Light, he further says, "is not any part of man's nature, nor yet any relic of any good which Adam lost by his fall." It is a "distinct, separate thing from man's soul and all the faculties of it." "It is not only distinct, but of a different nature from the soul of man and its faculties." It is to be distinguished even from "man's natural conscience, for conscience being that in man which ariseth from the natural faculties of man's soul may be defiled and corrupted."[15]

The Divine Light is thus wholly supernatural and put into man by a miraculous act, similar to that which sacramentarians attribute to the supernatural transubstantiation of bread and wine by which these elements are changed into the Divine body and blood of Christ, and which furnish the soul with "Grace." This Seed or Light becomes, in Barclay's own words, a *vehiculum Dei*[16]—a supernatural vehicle, or device, by which a distant God can operate in a soul that of its own nature has no spiritual capacity. This Light is placed in the soul at its creation, as "a spiritual Seed," after the same manner as innate ideas were supposed by Descartes to be injected by God into the substance of the soul. The supernatural Seed lies, "as a real substance," hidden away and dormant in the natural soul, as naked grain lies in barren, stony ground.[17] The natural man can "resist" this Seed, even slay and crucify it, *or* he can "receive it in his heart," "suffer it to bring forth its natural and proper effect, until Christ be formed and raised within the soul, as the new man,"[18]—and this is salvation.

The division of natures, the dualism between God and man, is here stated as sharply and violently as it can be stated. His initial account of man compels Barclay to resort to a supernatural scheme by which everything that can be called "spiritual" is derived from the other world and is no part of man. Barclay is strongly opposed to the doctrine of the damnation of infants and to the election scheme of Calvin, but it is not easy to see how he logically avoids these two unpleasant conclusions. If a child has nothing "spiritual" in his own nature and can become "spiritual" only by actively and voluntarily receiving the Seed into his heart and suffering it to grow and develop within him, and he dies before he has arrived at a capacity to do this, he would appear—unless a miracle is worked somewhere else—to remain for ever unspiritual and so unsaved. Again, it is difficult to see why, when we are all alike unspiritual and depraved by nature, some of us receive and respond to this "Seed" and so become saved, while the rest of us never do respond to it but go on living as if it had not been hidden in our nature. None of us can save ourselves, and yet some are saved and some are not. The "election" is somehow a mysterious fact. Barclay implies that it is due to the fact that God visits some at favoured seasons and does not in the same way visit others. There are some persons, he positively admits, who receive Grace[19] in such a measure and with such prevailing power that they cannot resist its saving operations. "In such a special manner He worketh in some, in whom Grace so prevaileth, that they necessarily obtain salvation; neither doth God suffer them to resist." If it is true that Divine Grace does in some instances manifest itself in irresistible prevailing power, one wonders why it works more feebly in others so that they can consequently resist its saving operation. The problem of free-will is difficult in any system of thought, and all theologians have found it hard to avoid some form of "election." Barclay supposed that he had escaped the net, but it is not obvious to the modern reader that he has done so. There is, of course, no way of securing or guaranteeing human freedom if it be taken for granted that the natural man is inherently and essentially unspiritual and incapable of any operations that contribute to the spiritual life. In fact, if man is wholly unspiritual by nature and can be saved in any case only by miracle, the lost would appear to be lost, not through man's conscious fault but because the miracle was not worked in their case or at least not worked sufficiently to save them.

But the graver difficulty with the entire scheme is found in the fact that we are left by this device with no criterion or test of truth. We are given in this foreign and supernatural Seed a religious principle which has no genuine ground in the nature of reason, and is incapable of correlation with reason. The Light, or Seed, is of a wholly different nature from the rational soul of man. It has no likeness or similarity to the natural faculties with which we are endowed, and by which we live our normal life. It is injected into man from another sphere, and is as foreign to our life as an archangel or seraph would be in our municipal politics. It is not commensurable with any native power of ours or with any facts or features of the world in which we are placed. It is not a product of experience. It is not the result of any known process. We possess nothing in our mental outfit by which we could ever pass judgment upon the pronouncements or the revelations of this Light. Only by miracle could the "openings" thus made to us from another sphere *fit* the scenery and circumstance of our natural world with its historical problems and its social issues. We are bound all the time to live and think and work with natural men and with societies of natural men, and we must face tasks that have grown out of natural sociological and ethical movements—and yet our only guide, beyond that of instinct and unspiritual reason, is a Light wholly distinct from and unrelated to the world where the concrete problems arise. This is as strange and as difficult to rationalize as was Descartes' double-world scheme, which absolutely sunders into two unrelated spheres the mind in man from the external world where man's life is lived. Descartes' scheme furnishes no basis for explaining how the mind inside can ever know any outside fact. Every act of knowledge becomes miraculous. So, too, in Barclay, every spiritual action is miraculous. Man could not do it if it were not done for him and through him. Man is thus treated as a thoroughfare through which distant mysterious forces, unlike any known forces in *this* world, supernaturally operate.

These intellectual difficulties, which have for many generations been allowed to pass unanalysed and unnoted, might well have been left still unchallenged were it not for the important fact that they have carried along through all these same generations grave historical consequences. Somewhere something happened which profoundly altered the entire character of the Quaker movement. Its mysticism shifted from the dynamic affirmation mysticism of the first period to a passive and negative type. A Quietism which nobody detects in the early days settled down upon it and utterly transformed it. It has been supposed that this Quietism came from the continent of Europe and was due to foreign influences. Friends did show great interest in continental Quietism, and were at a later time strongly influenced by it, but the unescapable fact remains that Friends had settled into a confirmed Quietism long before they discovered and used the writings of the great Quietists of France and Italy.

It will not do, of course, to attribute the appearance of Quietism in the Quaker movement to one sole influence. Group-attitudes and habits are subtle things and can seldom be traced to one isolated cause. But it is a plain and patent fact that Barclay's formulation is charged and loaded with the essential conditions and tendencies of Quietism. The entire basis and framework of Quietism are already there.

All forms of Quietism start with a despair of the natural man. They begin with a recognition of the spiritual bankruptcy of mere man. Every spiritual step, every act that has to do with religion and salvation, Quietism maintains, must be done in man by some Divine power beyond him. *His* only part in the transaction is a passive part. He ceases to resist the operations of God, and waits in quiet for "visitations," and for the coming of supernatural assistance. One does not need to turn to the continental Quietists for this teaching; it is all in Barclay, and is vividly and emphatically expressed there.

As we have seen, Barclay holds that natural man is "miserable," "depraved," and "unspiritual"—"without capacity for salvation." Every spiritual act of every sort is performed in man by a Divine *vehiculum* detached from his own nature and working through him. Man's only part and sole contribution is passivity. His one single function in spiritual matters is not to resist the Divine seed, the imparted grace. "He that resists it not, it becomes his salvation: so that in him that is saved the working is of the *grace* [used for 'Seed' and 'Light'], and not of the man; and it is a passiveness rather than an act."[20] Barclay continues: "The first step is not by man's working, but by his not contrary working." At the "singular seasons of man's visitation," "man is wholly unable of himself to work with the grace [*i.e.* co-operate], neither can he move one step out of his natural condition, until the grace [the superadded power] lay hold upon him; so it is possible for him to be passive and not to resist it, as it is possible for him to resist it. So we say, the grace of God works in and upon man's nature, which *though of itself wholly corrupted and defiled and prone to evil*, yet is capable to be wrought upon by the grace of God."[21] There is thus no co-operation between man and the superadded grace. It works in its own way, accomplishes its own end. Man's only act is a decision to lie passive and not resist it. Man of himself is powerless to bring about a "visitation"—"he must," as Barclay says, "wait for it." "He cannot move and stir [it] up when he pleaseth; but it moves, and strives with man as the Lord seeth meet." "It comes at certain times and seasons, and he must wait for it."[22] That is the essential basis, the distinguishing mark of Quietism. Barclay's letters, especially those to the Princess Elizabeth, and his theological writings generally, use very often the Quietistic phrase, "pure love," "pure light," "pure or naked truth," "pure motion," by which he means the "love," or "light," or "truth," or "influence" Divinely imparted to the soul without any admixture at all of the human. He does not write to Elizabeth until he has a "pure" moving to do so: "I was not willing to do anything in the forwardness of my own spirit," and he adds: "I shall be glad to hear from thee as thou finds *true freeness* to let me know how things are with thee."[23] His proposal of marriage to Christian Molleson contains a similar Quietistic note: "I can say in the fear of the Lord that I have received a charge from Him to love thee."[24]

There is, however, unfortunately, no safe and sound way on this basis of "pure truth" of discriminating between the true Divine motion and the motion which has a human and subjective origin. Reason has been ruled out as the arbiter. Experience is not admitted as the test. The Divine intimation, or pure moving, is supposed to be its own sure evidence, but we are never told by what infallible sign its Divine origin can be recognized. On a certain occasion Barclay himself felt impelled by an inward moving, which he felt to be "pure," to put on sackcloth, to cover his head with ashes, and to go through the streets of Aberdeen, crying to the people to repent. His own account of the strange incident, given in *A Seasonable Warning* is as follows:

" . . . The Command of the Lord concerning this thing came unto me that very Morning, as I awakened, and the Burthen thereof was very great; yea, seemed almost insupportable unto me, (for such a thing, until that very Moment, had never entered me before, not in the most remote Consideration.) And some, whom I called to declare to them this thing, can bear Witness, how great was the Agony of my Spirit, how I besought the Lord with Tears, that this Cup might pass away from me! Yea, how the Pillars of my Tabernacle were shaken, and how exceedingly my Bones trembled, until I freely gave up unto the Lord's Will."

This well illustrates the difficulty involved in this Quietistic theory. There is no test, no criterion. The moving is its own evidence. One must not question *why*, one must not ask for rational grounds. Reason is excluded. One must simply obey. But the mind of man is such a curious thing, with its subliminal suggestions, its morbid whisperings, its dreams and imaginings, its imitations and its auto-possessions, that it is never quite possible to assume that "movings" which burst with force into the sphere of the mind are on their own evidence "pure" and supernatural. Barclay admits that "the devil might form a sound of words, convey it to the outward ear and deceive the outward senses, by making things appear that are not."[25] It would seem, then, that this malicious spirit might even more easily inwardly deceive the most sincere and devout soul.

Quietism, having eliminated reason, has never told its adherents how to discriminate between the false light and the true. On its presuppositions there is no answer to the question. The Divine and the human belong to two different worlds and the higher cannot be tested and verified by anything in our lower world.

One who studies with care and insight the history of Quakerism through the two centuries succeeding Barclay's formulation will see that many of the tragedies and many of the internal difficulties have sprung out of this assumed spiritual bankruptcy of man and this Quietistic contrivance for obviating it. All the controversies of later Quaker history involve Barclay. The development of each new issue has been made in reference to his positions. He was a sort of John Brown of the entire period of Quaker struggle. He died before the internal conflicts began, but his soul went moving on through the whole of them. If he had shaped the issues differently the entire trend of Quaker history would have been another matter. No Friend appeared for two hundred years who could give, or at least who did give, a searching examination of this interpretation of the fundamental basis of Quakerism and with one consent it was accepted as the final authority. The great controversialists, Elias Hicks and his orthodox opponents;

Joseph John Gurney and John Wilbur; the Beaconites and their opposers, all took Barclay's account of "the natural man" as though there were no further word to say about it. Their differences were upon the question of how God had met this existing crisis and how under prevailing conditions salvation could be accomplished. They never got beneath the ancient presuppositions. The deeper questions of the real nature of God and man and their fundamental relation to one another never got adequate treatment. We find nobody breaking loose and going down to the deeper level.

Robert Barclay is not to be blamed for the historical tragedy. The formulators of truth in any field are bound to use the psychology and metaphysics of their age. They must think, if they think at all, through the terminology of their time and in the concepts that prevail around them, and they invariably determine the line of march of human thought and even fix in advance the kind of intellectual questions that will be asked in succeeding periods.

What I regret most is that the early formulation of Quakerism should have been made as an adjustment with the Augustinian and Calvinistic system instead of following the fresh and transforming path which the spiritual reformers, the real forerunners and progenitors of "the Children of the Light," had discovered. That latter course would have meant a different history and, I believe, a greater career for the movement—a real day-dawn and day-star rising for spiritual religion.

One other adjustment to the demands of the world and external history calls for a few words of comment in this Introduction—the adjustment to the State. When Quakerism burst in upon the world, its leaders took no account of consequences. They had, they believed, received an "opening," a revelation, which had complete right of way. Everything else must stand aside for it, or at least take second place. The "truth" which possessed their souls involved a new venture of life, and they were ready to risk reputation, home, family, goods, and life in their holy experiment. They had no thought

of compromising at any point, of yielding any ground or bend-
ing around any obstacles, or of ceasing the *fight*—they would
have said ceasing to "bear their testimony"—

> Till [they should build] Jerusalem
> In England's green and pleasant land.[26]

This rebel-attitude toward existing situations, this unyielding
spirit, produced, as it always does, a remarkable type of person
and a highly dynamic and incalculable movement. George
Whitehead and those who joined with him in the patient
work of securing "tolerations" and "privileges" for Friends
were, without knowing it, preparing for a different type of
person and were passing over from a movement charged with
potential energy to a stage of arrested development and cooling
enthusiasm. Once more we cannot blame these sincere ad-
justers. They wanted to secure their right to life, liberties,
and, if not "the pursuit of happiness," at least the privilege
to worship God as their hearts dictated. Why should they
go on fighting further with their spiritual weapons if kindly-
minded sovereigns and tolerant parliaments were ready to
grant them a large measure of the claims for which they had
suffered so much?

What they hardly realized, however, was the subtle though
fundamental change of ground. The "Children of the Light"
in their day had not been concerned for rights and privileges
for themselves and were not concerned to establish claims of
their own. They were champions of a universal truth; they
were the bearers of a faith for the whole human race; they
were contending for a new way of life for the entire world.
To secure a modicum of their "truth" and to win the privilege
of practising it by themselves within the peaceful area of
their own homes and meeting-houses would have seemed to
them no victory at all. They were the commissioned "apostles"
of a new order, and there could be no stopping-place until the
new kingdom was built. George Whitehead was a good man,
and he was a real success in securing happy adjustments, but
he marks, nevertheless, the end of an era, and is in his own

person the exhibition of a changed ideal.

History itself is a revelation of God. Its processes are sometimes stern and tragic. Its judgments are often severe. But it is always cathartic and clarifying. It arouses attention. It awakens consciousness. It drives home great realities. It demonstrates moral laws. It unveils the truth and it makes the fact of God's immanent presence as sure and certain as it can be made ni a world like ours. This history deals with one small human movement, covering only a fragment of time, but, even so, it is, like all genuine history, charged with spiritual significance and will bring the patient reader an illuminating message of the way God works in the world.

NOTES

1. *The Later Periods of Quakerism.*
2. *Sämmtliche Werke* (Erlangen edn.), xxii. p. 20.
3. *Paradoxa*, Vorrede, Sect. 45.
4. *Journal* (bi-cent. edn., 1891), i. 2.
5. These passages are found in Proposition iv. of the *Apology.*
6. *Apology*, Prop. iv. Part I. sect. 2.
7. For Calvin's account of "the Seed of Sin" see the *Institutes*, Book II. chap. i.
8. Whichcote's *Aphorisms*, 444.
9. A. Seth Pringle-Pattison's *The Idea of God*, p. 254.
10. D. G. Rossetti, Sonnet 37, "The Choice."
11. *Apology*, Prop. v. and vi. sect. 1.
12. *Ibid.* Stated in the original form of the Proposition vi. and expanded in sections 4 and 25.
13. *Ibid.* Prop. v. and vi. sect. 10.
14. *Ibid.* Prop. v. and vi. sect. 11, Consequence 6th.
15. *Ibid.* Prop. v. and vi. sect. 16.
16. *Ibid.* Prop. v. and vi. sect. 15, Quest. 5.
17. *Ibid.* Prop. v. and vi. sect. 14.
18. *Ibid.* Prop. v. and vi. sect. 13.
19. *Ibid.* Prop. v. and vi. sect. 18.
20. *Ibid.* Prop. v. and vi. sect. 17.
21. *Ibid.* Prop. v. and vi. sect. 17.
22. *Ibid.* Prop. v. and vi. sect. 16.
23. Letter to Princess Elizabeth, 27th of 4th mo. 1676.
24. See M. Christabel Cadbury's *Robert Barclay* (London, 1912), p. 33.
25. *Apology*, Prop. ii. sect. 6.
26. William Blake, "Jerusalem."

5

The Quakers in the American Colonies

AMERICAN Quakerism is closely bound up in origin and history with the wider religious movement which had its rise in the English Commonwealth, under the leadership of George Fox.[1] This type of religion, which took root in the American Colonies in 1657, and which grew to be a significant and far-reaching influence in at least ten Colonies, had already for ten years been powerfully stirring the middle classes, and had rapidly gathered numbers in the English counties. When the volunteers went forth for "the mighty work in the nations beyond the seas," as they expressed their mission, they were the representatives of an expanding body of believers at home, the executives of a matured policy of spiritual conquest, and they went forth to their "hardships and hazards" with an organised financial support behind them.[2] They felt, as their own testimony plainly shows, that they were not solitary adventurers, but that God was pushing them out to be the bearers of a new and mighty word of Life which was to remake the world, and that the whole group behind them was in some sense embodied in them. Throughout all the years during which the campaign of spiritual conquest was being pushed forward, the entire Society in England was pledged to the task of carrying its "truth" into the life of the New World, and even as early as 1660 George Fox was planning for the founding of a colony in America, where Quakers could try their faith and work out their ideals unmolested.[3] A study of Fox's printed *Epistles* will convince any one that the "Seed in America" was always prominent in his thought and in his plans.[4] In fact no other religious body in the Old World more completely identified itself with the fortunes of its apostles in the New World than did the Quakers, then in the youth and vigour of their career.

Throughout the entire period covered by this history— 1656 to 1780—Quakerism was an expanding force in the Colonies, and there were times within this period when it seemed destined to become one of the foremost religious factors in the life and development of America. It is clearly evident from their own writings that at the opening of the eighteenth century the Quaker leaders *expected* to make their type of religion prevail on the Western continent. They believed, in fact, that their "Principle" was universally true and would make its way through the race, and that their experiment was only the beginning of a world-religion of the Spirit. The New World seemed to them a providential field to be won for their truth. It was in the New World alone that favourable opportunities offered in the seventeenth and eighteenth centuries for the application of Quaker ideals to public life, and the opportunities were quickly seized. In Great Britain there were insuperable bars which kept Quakers out of public service to the state and forced them to adopt a life apart from the main currents. One famous Quaker, John Archdale, who took a prominent part in the making of three American Colonies— Maine, North Carolina and South Carolina—was elected to the English Parliament in 1698, but his refusal to take an oath cost him his seat, and ended all attempts on the part of Quakers to enter the field of politics. In America the situation was quite different. In the Puritan Colonies of New England, Quakers were, of course, without the privileges of franchise or office-holding, and in Episcopalian Colonies like Virginia, where uniformity was insisted upon, the way to influence in the government was tightly closed to them; but in Rhode Island the only obstacle to position in Government affairs which the Quakers met was the difficulty of bearing responsibility for war-preparation. In that Colony for more than a hundred years Quakers were continually in office, and for thirty-six terms the Governorship of the colony was occupied by members of the Society. In Pennsylvania they had one of the largest and most influential Colonies of the New World in their own hands. They came into possession of West Jersey in 1674, and five years later East Jersey also passed into their hands, so that they had the governmental control of New Jersey until it became a royal Colony.

Until 1701 they were the only organised religious denomination in North Carolina, and the administration of the Quaker, John Archdale, profoundly shaped the history of both Carolinas. Naturally Quakers in the Old World looked to the New as a land of promise, and no pains were spared to spread the "Seed" in the favourable regions along the Atlantic coast, so that by the middle of the eighteenth century there were more Quakers in the Western hemisphere than in Great Britain. They formed half the population of Newport in 1700 and for many years after, and down to the middle of the eighteenth century they were a majority of the population of the South Narragansett shore of Rhode Island, now Washington County. There were at this period three thousand Quakers in the southern section of Massachusetts, once the territory of the Pilgrim Fathers. About one-third of the inhabitants in the Piscataqua region of Maine and New Hampshire were Quakers. Lynn, Salem, Newbury, and Hampton had large Meetings, and many of the inland rural districts of Massachusetts and Rhode Island were predominantly Quaker. They formed a large proportion of the Long Island towns and the towns of Westchester County on the mainland, and by the middle of the century they constituted an influential body in New York City. There were not less than twenty-five thousand Quakers in Pennsylvania before the end of our period, and probably not far from six thousand in New Jersey. There were by official figures three thousand in Maryland, probably four or five thousand in Virginia, and about the same number in the Carolinas. They were thrifty, prosperous, and quiet in their modes of life, but contributing their share of the hard labour which turned the dense forests into flourishing fields, and their share also of those subtler formative forces which prepared the way in the wilderness for a great national life, then hardly dreamed of. It is no doubt a home-spun narrative, but history is no longer aristocratic. It does not confine its purview to selected heroes and purple-tinted events. It has become interested in the common man and in plain every-day happenings, and this story, though modest, is a contribution to the real life of America.

The extent of the Quaker influence in the political life of the Colonies has not been generally realised. The "holy experiment" of Penn had striking and dramatic features which have always impressed the imagination, but the quieter work of New England and Carolina Quakers has received much less notice and has waited long for a historian. But while emphasising this neglected field of Quaker activity, we must not lose our perspective and balance. The Quakers' supreme passion was the cultivation of inward religion and an outward life consistent with the vision of their souls. "Experiments in government" whether successful or unsuccessful, whether wise or unwise, were never their primary aim. Beneath these ventures, there always existed a deeper purpose—to make a fresh *experiment in spiritual religion*—as the living pulse of all Quaker aspiration, and by this central aim the movement must be finally estimated and judged. These American Quakers of the period here studied believed, with a white-hot intensity, that they had discovered, or rediscovered, a new spiritual Principle which they thought was destined to revolutionise life, society, civil government, and religion. The Principle (and they always spelled it with a capital P) which they claimed to have discovered was the presence of a Divine Light in man, a radiance from the central Light of the spiritual universe, penetrating the deeps of every soul, which if responded to, obeyed, and accepted as a guiding star, would lead into all truth and into all kinds of truth. They thought that they had found a way to the direct discovery of the Will of God and that they could thereby put the Kingdom of God into actual operation here in the world. The whole momentous issue of life, they insisted, is settled by personal obedience or disobedience to the inward Divine revelation. The wisdom of the infinite God

is within reach of the feeblest human spirit; the will of the
Eternal is voiced in the soul of every man; it is life to hear and
obey; it is death to follow other voices. This underlying conception forms the spring and motive of all the distinctive activities of the colonial Quakers. They risked everything they
had on the truth of this Principle, and they must be judged by
the way in which they worked out their experiment in religion.
They were champions of causes which seemed new and dangerous to those who heard them, but behind all their propaganda there was one live central faith from which everything
radiated—the faith that God speaks directly to the human
spirit, and that religion, to be true and genuine, must be a
reality of first-hand experience.

There have been many individuals in the Christian Church
who have been exponents of this mystical idea that God manifests Himself inwardly to the soul of man and that His real
presence can be directly, immediately, *experienced*. The testimony of such mystics has profoundly interested our generation
and their experiences have received searching psychological
examination at the hands of experts.[5] The novel and interesting thing about this Quaker experiment is that it furnishes
an opportunity to study inward mystical religion embodied
in a group and worked out through a long span of historical
development. We shall here see the intense personal faith of
one or a few fusing an entire group and creating an atmosphere, a climate, into which children were born and through
which they formed their lives; we shall be able to study the
effect of the cooling processes of time on this faith so intense
at its origin; we shall discover how this startlingly bold Principle met the slow siftings and testings of history; and we
shall find out how any merely inward and mystical facts must
be supplemented and corrected by the wider concrete and objective experience of the race.

It is true, no doubt, that religion is in the last analysis a
personal matter, but it is also true that nobody cut apart from
social interests and isolated from the purposes and strivings of
a group of fellows could become a *person* at all, or could ex-

hibit what we mean by religion. And, therefore, while we go to biography for our most definite accounts of religious experience, it is through the unfolding of history that we can trace out the full significance of a first-hand faith like the one here in question, and only in the vast laboratory of history, where every hypothesis must submit to a stern test, can it be fairly verified or transcended. The following chapters as they unfold will present the Quaker Principle in sufficient detail, will exhibit it in sharp collision with other views, and will show its points of strength and weakness; but a few clues indicated here in the Introduction will perhaps help the reader to find his way more easily and more intelligently.

1. One point which this volume will clearly settle is the fact that there existed in the Colonies, before the arrival of the Quaker missionaries, a large number of persons, in some instances more or less defined groups of persons, who were seeking after a freer and more inward type of religion than that which prevailed in any of the established Churches.

The period of the English Commonwealth witnessed an extraordinary revival of faith in man's power to discover the inward way to God, and mystical sects, some of them wise and sane, some of them foolish and fanatical, swarmed almost faster than they could be named. These mystical sectaries had one idea in common: they believed that God was in man and that revelation was not closed. They were waiting for the dawn of a fresh Light from heaven.[6] Wherever English Colonists of this period went these sectaries went too. They were a constant annoyance to New England Puritans, to Dutch Calvinists, and to Virginia Churchmen. They generally gathered kindred spirits around them and quietly—or sometimes noisily —propagated their mystical faith. They exalted personal experience, direct intercourse with God, and so put much less stress than their neighbours did upon the forms and doctrines which had come to be regarded as essential elements of a sound and stable faith. This was the prepared soil in which Quakerism spread at its first appearing, and without which the efforts of the propagators, however valiant, would almost certainly have been futile. The Quaker missionaries simply gave positive direction to tendencies already powerfully underway. They brought to clear focus ideas which were before vague and indefinite, and they fused into white heat spirits that were feeling after and dimly seeking what they now heard in their own tongue. The first "Quaker Churches" in America were formed out of this sort of material; and so too were many of the Meetings which came into being at later periods of expansion.

2. One of the first tasks which confronts the historian who proposes to deal with the religious life of the Colonies—especially of the New England Colonies—is to understand and fairly estimate the collision between the Puritans and the Quakers. In many respects they were both the product of a common movement, the spiritual offspring of the same epoch. They both possessed a passion for righteousness—a moral earnestness—that hardly has a historical parallel except in the great Hebrew prophets. They both took a very pronounced stand against "natural pleasures," enjoyments of "the world" and of "the flesh," in fact against actions of any kind along the line of least resistance. They were both opposed to fashions and customs which fostered, in any way, looseness of life, or which ministered, in any degree, to personal pride and selfishness. In short, they were both "puritan," in the ancient sense of the word, in their moral basis and in their conception of social proprieties. They both hated tyranny with an intense hatred, though they took very different ways of destroying it; and they both abhorred sacerdotalism in religion, though they drew the line where sacerdotalism began at very different points.

But if they were allied in spirit in some common elemental aspects, they were nevertheless exponents of very antagonistic types of religion which, seen from the different angles of vision and perspective, were absolutely irreconcilable, and it was still the fashion then to count it sin to be weak in infallibility. Our generation is so open-minded and hospitable, so weaned of the taste of finality-doctrines, that we look almost with amazement at these exponents of the fiery positive, these tournaments to settle which "infallible truth" really *was* infallible. We must, however, always bear in mind that religious indifference is a distinctly modern trait. The testimony of the Rev. Mr. Ward of Ipswich, Massachusetts, in 1645, might be paralleled in almost any ecclesiastical writing of that period: "It is said that men ought to have liberty of conscience and that it is *persecution* to debar them of it. I can rather stand amazed than reply to this. It is an astonishment that the brains of a man should be parboiled in such impious ignorance." John Callender, writing of the freedom established in the little Colony on the island of Rhode Island says with much truth: "In reality the true Grounds of Liberty of Conscience were not then [1637] known, or embraced by any Sect or Party of Christians; all parties seemed to think that as they only were in possession of the Truth, so they alone had a right to restrain and crush all other opinions, which they respectively called Error and Heresy, where *they* were the most numerous and powerful."[7]

Here in the same field were two exponents of the "fiery positive," both profoundly, sincerely conscious of the infallible truth of their convictions, and with their lives staked upon divergent and irreconcilable conceptions of Divine revelation. For the Puritan, revelation was a miraculous projection of God's Word and Will from the supernatural world into this world. This "miraculous projection" had been made only in a distinct "dispensation," through a limited number of Divinely chosen, specially prepared "instruments," who received and transmitted the pure Word of God. When the "dispensation" ended, revelation came to a definite close. No word more could be added, as also none could be subtracted. All spiritual truth for the race for all ages was now unveiled; the only legitimate function which the man of God could henceforth exercise was that of *interpretation*. He could declare what the Word of God meant and how it was to be applied to the complicated affairs of human society. Only a specialist in theology could, from the nature of the case, be a minister under this system. The minister thus became invested with an extraordinary dignity and possessed of an influence quite *sui generis*.

For the Quaker, revelation was confined to no "dispensation"—it had never been closed. If any period was peculiarly "the dispensation of the Holy Spirit," the Quaker believed that it was the present in which he was living. Instead of limiting the revelation of the Word of God to a few miraculous "instruments," who had lived in a remote "dispensation," he insisted that God enlightens every soul that comes into the world, communes by His Holy Spirit with all men everywhere, illuminates the conscience with a clear sense of the right and the wrong course in moral issues, and reveals His Will in definite and concrete matters to those who are sensitive recipients of it. The true minister, for the Quaker of that period, was a *prophet* who spoke under a moving and by a power beyond his human powers, and so was, in fresh and living ways, a *revealer* of present truth, and not a mere interpreter of a past revelation. The Quaker "meeting" was, in theory at least, a continuation of Pentecost—an occasion for the free blowing of the Spirit of God on men. It was plainly impossible in the seventeenth century for those two types of Christianity to live peaceably side by side. A tragic collision was inevitable.

3. There is another problem in Quaker history no less urgent than the problem of collision with divergent conceptions of truth, and that is the strange fact that a movement so full of vitality and power at its origin ceased to expand with the expanding life of America. So long as the "tragic collisions" lasted, the Quakers flourished and seemed sure of a significant future in the unfolding spiritual life of America; as soon as they were free and unopposed there occurred a slowing-down and a loss of dynamic impact on the world. No treatment of colonial Quakerism can be adequate which fails to face this somewhat depressing fact, for the historian who presents the assets and achievements of a movement is under obligation to

deal squarely as well with its liabilities, weaknesses, and failures.

The thing which above everything else doomed the movement to a limited and subordinate role was the early adoption of the ideal that Quakers were to form a "peculiar people." In the creative stage of the movement the leaders were profoundly conscious that they had discovered a universal truth which was to permeate humanity, and form, by its inherent demonstration and power, a World-Church—the Church of the living God. It was in that faith and in the inspiration of that great idea that the pioneer missionaries went forth. Then gradually, at first unconsciously, in the face of a very stubborn world that not only was not persuaded, but further went positively to work to suppress the alleged "fresh revelation," the movement underwent a radical change of ideal. The aim slowly narrowed down to the formation of a "spiritual remnant," set apart to guard and preserve "the truth" in the midst of a crooked and perverse generation that would not see and believe. The world-vision faded out, and the attention focused on "Quakerism" as an end-in-itself. The transformation which occurred in this case has many striking parallels in the history of other spiritual experiments. The living *idea* organises a definite Society for the propagation of it, and lo, the Society unconsciously smothers the original idea and becomes absorbed in itself! It is a very ancient tragedy, and that tragedy happened again here in this movement. The transformation is written large on the Records of the Meetings and in the Journals of the leaders. "Truth" soon came to be a definite, static thing. No creed was made and no declaration of faith was adopted, but a well-defined body of Quaker conceptions soon came into shape, and came also into habitual use. Not only did the ideas of the Society crystallise into static concepts of truth, the form of worship too became fixed and well-nigh unalterable. There was no "programme" of service and no positive prearrangement, but it was soon settled that silence was the essential "form" for true worship, and that spiritual ministry must be spontaneous, unpremeditated, and of the "prophetic" type.

The primitive aim at simplicity and the desire to escape from slavery to fashion underwent a corresponding change and dropped to the easy substitute of a fixed form of dress and speech, which soon became itself a kind of slavery. A definite attitude toward music and art and "diversions" in general was adopted so that individuals might be relieved of the difficulty, and incidentally of the danger, of personal decision. Marriage with "the world's people" was made as difficult as it possibly could be made. In short, a Quaker became a well-marked and definitely-labelled individual—quite as rigidly *set* as any of the "religious orders" of Church history and quite as bent on preserving the peculiar type. Men spent their precious lives, not in propagating the living principles of spiritual religion in the great life of the world, but in perfecting and transmitting a "system" within the circle of the Society, and the heart-burnings and tragedies which mark the lives of the consecrated men and women who, in these days, bore the ark, were too often concerned with the secondary rather than with the primary things of spiritual warfare. The martyrdoms for the world-cause were heroic, dramatic, and of universal interest; these later travails and tragedies often seem petty, trivial, and unnecessary, and they make a very limited appeal to human interest.

The movement was hampered from the start, and in every stage of its history during the period of this volume by the imperfect conception of the Inward Light, and of the whole relation between the Divine and the human, which was consciously or unconsciously adopted. This was perhaps inevitable, as every movement is necessarily more or less bound up with the prevailing ideas, the intellectual climate, of the age in which it takes its rise. In the seventeenth and early eighteenth centuries a dualistic universe was taken for granted. There was a sharp distinction, a wide chasm, between the "natural" and the "supernatural." The urgent question with everybody was—not how *the entire universe from material husk to spiritual core could be unified and comprehended as an organic whole,* but how the chasm which sundered the two worlds could be miraculously bridged. It is not our problem to-day, but it was the one the Quaker was facing. His opponents said that the chasm was bridged by a miraculous communication of the Word of God in a definite and finished Revelation. *He* said that it was bridged by the communication of a super-natural Light given to each soul. The trouble was that he never could succeed in bringing into unity the two things assumed to be sundered. On the one hand there was the "mere man," whom he assumed, as everybody else did, to be, in his natural condition, non-spiritual and incapable of doing any-thing toward his own salvation; and on the other a Divine Light, or Seed of God, projected into this "natural man" as the illuminating, saving, and revealing Principle in him. The Light was distinctly conceived as something supernatural and foreign to man as man—something added to him as a gift.

With this basic conception for his working theory, the Quaker naturally and logically looked upon the true minister as a passive and oracular "instrument" of the Holy Spirit. His message, in so far as it was "spiritual," was believed to come "through him and from beyond him." He was not a teacher or an interpreter, he was a "revealer" through whom Divine truth was "opened." The direct result of such a view, of course, was that human powers were lightly esteemed and quite distrusted. Instead of having a principle which brought the finite being, with all his potential powers, into organic union with the self-revealing, co-operating God, thus pro-ducing a spiritual, developing, autonomous personality, with an incentive to expand all its capacities, he had a funda-mental conception which tended toward a distrust and sup-pression of the native powers. Spiritual messages, instead of being thought of as the contribution which a person himself makes when he is raised to his highest and best by co-oper-ation with the Divine Spirit in whom his finite life is rooted, were thought of as messages oracularly "given" to him—his part being simply that of a transmitter.

The human element in man's spiritual activities was discounted and almost eliminated in order to heighten the Divine aspect, as in an earlier theology the human element in Christ had been suppressed to exalt His divinity. That this unpsychological theory worked out badly in practice there can be no question in the mind of anybody who studies the movement historically; but it only means that they were unsuccessful and unhappy in their way of *formulating* their theory of Divine and human intercourse. What they wanted to say was that God and men were in direct correspondence, and that man at his best could lay hold of life and light and wisdom and truth which ordinarily transcends his narrow finite self. Of such heightened correspondence there is plenty of evidence. The only pity is that their wrongly-formulated theory so often stood in their way and hampered them and prevented them from a normal use of all their capacities.

Their failure to appreciate the importance of the fullest expansion of human personality by education is the primary cause of their larger failure to win the commanding place in American civilisation of which their early history gave promise. Their central Principle, properly understood, called for a fearless education, for there is no safety in individualism, in personal responsibility, or in democracy, whether in civil or religious matters, unless every individual is given a chance to correct his narrow individualism in the light of the experience of larger groups of men. If a man is to be called upon to follow "his Light," he must be helped to correct his *subjective seemings* by the gathered objective wisdom of the race, as expressed in scientific truth, in historical knowledge, in established institutions, and in the sifted literature of the world. The Quaker ideal of ministry, too, calls for a broad and expansive education even more than does that of any other religious body. If the particular sermon is not to be definitely prepared, then the person who is to minister must *himself* be prepared. If he is to avoid the repetition of his own petty notions and commonplace thoughts he must form a richer and more comprehensive experience from which to draw,

> For every fiery prophet in old times,
> And all the sacred madness of the bard,
> When God made music thro' them, could but speak
> His music by the framework and the chord.[8]

George Fox had moments of insight into the importance of this objective element, and in a great sentence he urged the founding of educational institutions for teaching everything "civil and useful in the creation"; but institutions of such scope unfortunately did not get founded. If there could have been established, in the northern, central, and southern sections of the Atlantic coast line, institutions adapted to the right education of Quaker youth, as Harvard and Yale were to the education of the Puritan youth, there would be quite another story to tell. As the problem *was* worked out, no adequate education for Quaker youth was available. They soon found themselves largely cut off from the great currents of culture, and they thus missed the personal enlargement which comes when one is forced to make his own ideals fit into larger systems of thought, and is compelled to reshape them in the light of facts. The absence of constructive leaders, the later tendency to withdraw from civic tasks, the relaxing of the idea of reshaping the world, which this history reveals, were due, in the main, to the lack of expansive education. The beautiful old-fashioned home passed on to the child who came into it the stock of truth and the definite ideals which were alive in it; it fed the growing mind with the literature which its people had produced, and the Meetings furnished a spiritual climate that was sweet and wholesome to breathe, but there was nothing to lift the youth up to a sight of new horizons. He was more or less *doomed* to the level of the past. The denominations that were training the fittest of their sons to become thinkers and leaders were sure sooner or later to win the birthright and to take away the blessing from the Quakers.

With the Revolutionary War there came a great awakening, which showed itself most definitely in a determination to provide larger opportunities for Quaker education. Steps were taken in each section of the country to provide for the education of the new generation. It was a fortunate awakening and it has led to great results, but it came too late to enable the Quakers to achieve the place in the civilisation of the Western world which their early history prognosticated. They were already being left behind, and were already accepting the view that they were to be a small and isolated sect—"a remnant" of God's people. The fateful years which were selecting the dominating religious forces of America were the years of colonial development, and during those eventful years the Quakers were not awake to the chance that was going by. Then, too, when the awakening did come, there was still a long period during which contracted ideals of education prevailed. Nobody seemed able to get beyond the narrow plan of "guarded education," which is not, in the true sense of the word, *education* at all. It is still only the transmission of certain well-defined and "safe" ideas and tends to produce uncreative and unconstructive minds. It is a well-meant plan for the propagation of an existing body of ideas, but it does not and cannot make large and forceful leaders and creators of fresh ideals.[9] The whole trend of the century before had been toward the preservation of a definite type and had fostered the timid attitude. It was not to be expected, when the awakening came, that there would be men ready for the bold experiment of a broad and fearless education which set the youth free, with open mind, to study everything "civil and useful in the creation," and which left him to make his own selection of what was to be truth for him. The Quaker has slowly found the road to that genuine type of education, but he has come to it late. Whether he now has recovering power enough to repair the damages of the past and can still realise the destiny which seemed his in the last half of the seventeenth century, is not a question to be answered here, but it is a fact that his failure to provide for an adequate education during the formative years lies at the base of his larger failure to *arrive*.[10]

4. In one particular respect the colonial Quakers made a

very important contribution to religion—they produced saints, and these saints were and remain the finest and most fragrant bloom of American Quakerism.

Sainte-Beuve has given, in his *Port Royal*, a penetrating account of persons who have been transformed into saintly life through the reception of Divine grace. "Such souls," he says, "arrive at a certain fixed and invincible state, a state which is genuinely heroic, and from out of which the greatest deeds are performed. . . . They have an inner state which before all things is one of love and humility, of infinite confidence in God, and of severity to themselves, accompanied with tenderness for others." This is an accurate account of the colonial Quaker saint—invincibly fixed in purpose, genuinely heroic, ready for great deeds, possessed of infinite confidence in God, and withal tender in love and humility. I am not sure that our busy and commercial age would call these saints "efficient"— they were not trained and equipped as modern social workers are—but they were triumphantly beautiful spirits, and the world still needs beautiful lives as much as it needs "efficient" ones, and the beautiful life in the long run is dynamic and does inherit the earth.[11]

These rare and beautiful souls, like great artistic creations of beauty, are not capable of explanation in utilitarian terms, nor can their origin be traced in terms of cause and effect, but it can safely be said that they never come except among people consecrated to the Invisible Church. It requires a pure and fervid devotion to the Pattern in the mount, a loyalty to the holy Jerusalem—the *urbs Sion mystica*—to fashion a Christian saint, whether Catholic or Quaker. No one can be wholly absorbed in the affairs of an actual earthly church without being marred by the politics of it, and without becoming small and narrow and provincial by reason of the limitations of locality and temporal climate. The saint belongs to an actual church, to be sure, loves it and serves it, but he keeps his soul set on the vision of the Church Invisible in which the saints of all ages are members with him, and in that vision he lives.

There must also be a loosening of the hold on "the world"

to prepare a saint of this type. There must at least be no rivalry to disturb the concentration of soul on eternal Realities. The very rigour of renunciation, the stern demands of a religion which cuts its adherents off from primrose paths of life, seem almost essential to the creation of this kind of saintliness. It is only by strict parallelism with celestial currents, only by drawing on invisible and inexhaustible resources of Grace, only by the cultivation of a finer spiritual perception than most possess that inward grace and central calm are achieved; only by stillness and communion that spiritual poise and power are won. There were, in the days of which I am writing, many Friends who had found the secret inner way into a real Holy of Holies. They had learned how to live from within outward, how to be refreshed with inward bubblings, how to walk their hard straight path with shining faces, though they wist not their faces did shine. The Quakers have no "calendar," no bead roll, and they have always been shy and cautious even of the word "saint," but almost every Meeting from Maine to South Carolina had during the period under review some persons who through help from Above refined and sublimated their nature and all unconsciously grew sweet and fragrant with the odour of saintly life.

5. One other positive contribution which they made to genuine spiritual religion remains to be catalogued—their contribution to the spread of lay-religion, by which I mean a form of religion dissociated from ecclesiasticism, and penetrating the life and activities of ordinary men. The real power of Quakerism lay in the quality of life produced in the rank and file of the membership. This history is weak, no doubt, in biographies of luminous leaders who rose far above the group and stood out as distinct peaks. Colonial Quakerism would have proved a barren field for a Carlyle, who assumed that history is the biography of heroes, raised by their genius head and shoulders above the level of their contemporaries. The real glory of this movement was the "levelling up" of an entire people. Farmers, with hands made rough by the plough-handle, in hundreds of rural localities not only

preached messages of spiritual power on meeting-days, but, what is more to the point, lived daily lives of radiant goodness in simple neighbourhood service. Women who had slight chances for culture, and who had to do the hard work of pioneer housewifery, by some subtle spiritual alchemy, were transformed into a virile sainthood which made its power felt both in the Sunday gathering and in the unordained care of souls throughout the community. It was a real experiment in the "priesthood of believers," and it was an incipient stage of what has become one of the most powerful spiritualising forces in our country—the unordained lay ministry of a vast multitude of men and women who have attacked every form of entrenched evil, and who, in city and country, are taking up the "cure of souls" with insight and efficiency.

It will be obvious to the reader that this book is not written from the point of view of the antiquarian. The historical facts have been carefully gathered, sifted, and verified, and they are as accurate as research could make them, but the central interest from first to last has been to discover how a group of men and women wrought out their souls' faith in an earlier century. They were persons who believed that within the deeps of themselves they touched the Infinite, that within their own spirits they could hear the living word of the Eternal. They believed this mighty thing, and they tried to make their belief real in life and word and deed. It is worth while perhaps even in this busy age to stop amid the din of commercial activity to see how plain people, raised to a kind of grandeur by their faith, tried to bring to the world once again a religion of life, and endeavoured to show that God is, as of old, an Immanuel God—with us and in us, the Life of our lives.

NOTES

1. The history of the rise of Quakerism has been written for this series by William Charles Braithwaite in the volume *The Beginnings of Quakerism*.
2. At a great General Meeting held at Scalehouse, near Skipton, in England, in 1658, an Epistle was issued which called for funds to push the work in

the Western world. The following extract indicates the spirit of the document: "Having heard of the great things done by the mighty power of God in many nations beyond the seas, whither He hath called forth many of our dear brethren and sisters to preach the everlasting gospel . . . our bowels yearn for them and our hearts are filled with tender love to those precious ones of God who so freely have given up for the Seed's sake their friends, their near relations, their country and worldly estates, yea and their lives also. We, therefore, with one consent freely and liberally offer up our earthly substance, according as God hath blessed every one—to be speedily sent up to London as a freewill offering for the Seed's sake." (The MS. of this Epistle is in the Library at Friends House, London, in Portfolio p. 16–1.)

3. Letter of Josiah Coale to George Fox from Maryland, January 1661. A. R. Barclay MSS. No. 53 at Friends House.

4. Fox's *Epistles* (first ed. 1698; American ed. 1831, 2 vols.).

5. James, *Varieties of Religious Experience;* Coe, *Spiritual Life;* Granger, *The Soul of a Christian;* Pratt, *The Psychology of Religious Belief;* Ames, *The Psychology of Religious Experience;* Delacroix, *Les Grands Mystiques chrétiens;* Inge, *Christian Mysticism;* Von Hügel, *The Mystical Element in Religion;* Evelyn Underhill, *Mysticism;* Jones, *Studies in Mystical Religion.*

6. See chapters xiv.–xx. of my *Studies in Mystical Religion.*

7. John Callender's *Historical Discourse* (Boston, 1739).

8. Tennyson's "Holy Grail."

9. "Guarded" is often used in another sense, namely, that young and tender children, while being educated, are to be shielded from immoral influences, which is, of course, highly commendable.

10. It must not be concluded because Quakerism did not flourish under these conditions and limitations that therefore its *spiritual ideal* has broken down. On the contrary, it has hardly yet been given an adequate trial.

11. John Woolman is the consummate flower of the type I have in mind. It was a saying of his that "some glances of real beauty may be seen in their faces who dwell in true meekness."

6

The Later Periods of Quakerism

The type of religion studied in the historical series of which these are the concluding volumes has been essentially mystical. No other large, organized, historically continuous body of Christians has yet existed which has been so fundamentally mystical, both in theory and practice, as the Society of Friends —the main movement studied in this series—from its origin in the middle of the seventeenth century until the end of the eighteenth century, and in certain sections even through the nineteenth century.

These present volumes record the profound transformation which occurred in the nineteenth century, and which carried a large proportion of the membership of the Society of Friends, both in England and America, over from a mystical basis to what for want of a better term may be called an evangelical basis. The process of transformation was very slow and came into operation—or at least to consciousness—long after the Wesleys and Whitefield had carried through their great evangelical revival; but though it was late, and though the main influence came from the evangelical leaders in the English Church rather than directly from the leaders of Methodism, there can be little question that this religious emphasis which was a characteristic feature of the Wesleyan revival, was the primary cause of the transformation of Quakerism. The transformation was, as I have said, gradual and proceeded for a long time without revealing the fact that a break with the past was taking place. It is clear, however, in historical perspective, that where the changes in the Society of Friends have been in the direction of a "return" to the evangelical systems of the reformed faith, a type of Christianity has been produced which is in strong and radical contrast to the mystical movement inaugurated by George Fox. The latter broke with the theological systems of Protestantism as completely as Luther and Calvin had done with Catholicism. He felt that he was inaugurating a *new reformation*. His movement was an attempt to produce a type of Christianity resting upon no authorities external to the human spirit, a Christianity springing entirely out of the soul's experience, verified and verifiable in terms of personal or social life. The simplification seemed possible to Fox and his friends because they had made the memorable discovery that the Christ who saves is a living Christ, operating in vital fashion within the lives of men. They had thus to do no longer with a system constructed on a theory of a God who was remote or absentee. They went forth with the *live conviction* that God, revealed to them in Christ, was active, creative and present—still making His world, so that they could expect new stages and fresh dawnings, even though the darkness seemed very thick and the dead hand of the past very heavy. To abandon that position and outlook and to "return" to the systems of the past would mean, of course, that Augustine and Luther and Calvin had won the victory and had triumphed over Fox, as in some sense and in some degree they have done.

In its broad and untechnical sense the adjective evangelical denotes a type of Christianity which conforms to the gospel of Jesus Christ, and which carries forward in a vital and dynamic way the life and message first expressed and proclaimed by Him and by the apostolic circle. Used in this untechnical sense, all devout believers in Jesus Christ, all of His true disciples and followers in all ages, are evangelicals, and none more truly so than the great mystics of the Christian Church. Those who, in the modern period, have joyously accepted the fresh light and the liberating influences brought to our age by scientific and historical research and who yet recognize the absolute spiritual supremacy of Christ, and who find in Him the full and final revelation of the essential nature of God and man, are, too, evangelicals in this proper and nobler meaning of the word. All great preaching—preaching, that is, which in our day or in any day convicts and trans-

forms men—owes its kindling power to its *evangelical note.*
Whenever an interpreter of Christianity returns to the heart
of the gospel message and recovers its life, its simplicity and
its authority, he becomes at once a moral and spiritual force
in his community and in his time. In all periods Friends have
aimed to be evangelical in this good sense of the word. They
have regarded the living Christ as the ground of their faith,
the source of their power, and the central fact of their message. They have proclaimed a positive and joyous evangel—
good news regarding God and man and the coming Kingdom.
Since the period of the Reformation, however, and more emphatically since the great awakening in the eighteenth century
under the leadership of Wesley, "evangelical" has taken on a
sharply defined and technical meaning. It denotes, in this
narrow sense, a well-marked conception of human nature, a
certain definite position toward the Scriptures, an essential
body of theological doctrine and an indispensable plan of
salvation. It stands in this latter sense not for a religious attitude or experience, but for the adoption of a definite theological system, belief in which is assumed to be essential to
salvation.

The vital task and mission of mysticism in all ages, whether
exhibited in individuals or in a group movement, like that of
the Society of Friends, has been to call men away from "theological systems," however sacred, to the fresh and living water
to be found in a personal experience of God. The mystic, when
once he has felt the joy of direct discovery of what life with
God means, cannot endure to think of reducing religion to an
affair of phrases or to a formulated scheme. It seems to him as
impossible to form and nurture the soul of man upon forensic
systems and theories of salvation as it would be to bring up a
child upon a book about mother-love. There are in either case
no adequate substitutes for the real thing.

Mysticism itself has not always avoided pitfalls and wandering fires. It has not always borne within itself the witness
and demonstration that new dimensions of life had been found
and that new sources of spiritual energy had been tapped. It

has, however, on the whole given a convincing testimony to the fact that the relation between God and man is not remote, forensic and logical, but direct, energizing, vital and transforming—as much a matter of experience and verification as sunlight is. The mystic has, of course, been compelled to use the language of his time, and he has often with reservations employed the expressions which the theologians have coined, but he has always refused to treat them as more than inadequate *symbols* and not to be substituted for the thrilling adventure of personal discovery.

The mystics have never consented to the view that the revelation of God is limited to an ancient dispensation or is confined to a Book. Their primary ground for believing that God once spoke through men—the men who wrote the Book —is their warm and intimate consciousness that the soul is still oracular and that God speaks now. They hold the revelation of God to be continuous and unending, though at the same time they put as great a value as any one does upon the ethical and spiritual truths revealed in the Bible. They are very conscious of human frailty. They know as much as any theologians do about sin and its dark trail over all our lives, but they nevertheless insist that the black blotches are on a white background, that man is made for divine companionship, that eternity has been put within our hearts, that evil is only one side of the human account, and that there is something—a homing instinct—in man which takes him back to God as naturally as the child turns in its joys and sorrows to its mother.

The interpretation which the mystic gives of salvation fits in essentially with this religion of experience and has in large measure sprung out of it. Christ, for the mystic, is the eternal Lover, the Bridegroom of souls. He is the crown and culmination of divine revelation, and in His life and person He has forever made visible and vocal in our world the mind, the will, the heart, the character of God. He is an eternal manifestation of God, striking His being into bounds at a definite period of history, being born in human form in time and space, living a

life of limitless love and forgiveness, and going the way of the
Cross in unspeakable agony of suffering that He might forever
show the consummate way of the spiritual life, and finally
triumphing over defeat and death in a resurrection which
proves Him to be a new type and order of spiritual life. He is
thus the head of a new race, the first of a new series, the
founder of a new kingdom, the revealer of a new way of living.
His divine love, wooing, pleading, appealing, enduring all
things, suffering with those who sin, and sharing the common
tragedies of life with us, is the power unto salvation for all
who understand and see its amazing significance. To be saved,
then, would be to live by the impact and inspiration of His
life, to feel the appeal of His personality, the contagion of His
spirit, the drawing force of His unspeakable love, the operation of His invisible and eternal presence within, making the
old life impossible and re-creating in the inner man a new will,
a new heart, a new mind and a new-natured self, so that the
old self with its instinctive tendencies no longer lives, but
Christ lives at the centre as the force and spring of action and
makes all things new.

The mystic here, as always, is assuming the immanence of
God—a one-world system in place of the two-world one. He
is oblivious to the chasm-theory. To put the supernatural
realm off yonder, beyond the world which we know and in
which we live, is to empty it of all value for explaining either
life or truth. If God is to be *our* God, He must be here in the
currents of life with us. Sin is to the mystic a fact, a tragic
fact, but it is due to finiteness, to ignorance, and to weakness
of will. Man must start from very feeble beginnings and learn
the way by slow and painful experience, by failures as well as
by successes. What he needs then is spiritual illumination and
moral re-enforcement. Christ is the source of both these. He
is the Light of Life. He reveals and exhibits life in its full and
complete measure. At last through Him we know what it
would be like to *live*. And He brings into operation the supreme moral energy—the power of an unparalleled love, a
love stronger than death, which neither height nor depth can

measure. This Friend of ours, who is at the same time the very Heart of God incarnated and revealed, has made us see what sin costs, and how immeasurably far divine love can go to bring us out of sin and to guide us through the mazes of the temporal stage to our true habitat. Salvation is thus for the mystic a vital thing. It is re-living the life of Christ in His power and by His spirit. It is not an act of forensic justification, it is a process of regeneration and transformation, and finally the attainment of the type of life of which Christ is the first and perfect example. To be saved is to have experienced a new creation.

The difference between this first type of religion and a type of religion on the other hand which insists upon the recognition and adoption of a set of doctrines is a very emphatic and cardinal difference. There is probably no existing religion which is completely reduced to formulation and system. In all great religious lives and in all powerful movements systems have been transcended, and experience has flowed over and inundated the narrow formulation. But there is a type of religion, nevertheless, which tends to terminate in a theological system, to lead up to a mighty scheme of salvation instead of bringing men to a living, loving Person who reveals to them the life for which they were made, and who influences them vitally and ethically rather than logically and forensically. Forms of religion which claim infallible authority are always of this second type. They assume that religion, to be religion, must be a supernatural addition to human life, and hence must come to man from another sphere, and must be mediated through some superhuman authority. They fail to realize the true divine and spiritual potentiality of man, and therefore their problem is at every step vastly different from that of a religion which begins and ends in direct experience of God as a normal fact of life.

Mystical religion, however, is not the only type that exhibits first-hand experience. It would be a mistake to imply that religion of the historical evangelical type has been, as revealed in lives, less dynamic and transforming than has mysticism. Both these types have been mighty spiritual forces in the day of their freshness and vitality, and they have both been as weak and ineffective as the shorn Samson in the cooled stage of crystallization and white ash. The evangelical movement of the eighteenth and nineteenth centuries, which finally came over into Quakerism, was of all things alive in the persons of its leaders and its saints, and, it must be added, alive also in the unnamed and forgotten ordinary, everyday people who in multitudes found a new hope and inspiration and power and moral purity through the gospel as the evangelical preachers interpreted it and proclaimed it. It was in its enkindled period no less a first-hand religion, no less a thing of experience, than was mysticism itself. What these men had discovered who woke England from its lethargy and changed sodden miners into clean-souled triumphant men and women was not a set of abstract dogmas to be argued about and printed in a book; they had found a personal Saviour whom they felt they knew, and who, as they trusted Him and followed Him, released them by a direct income of energy from their old habits and their former propensities. Whitefield, who certainly in temperament was not a mystic, and who looked for his salvation wholly to a finished work done for him by Another, had "a glorious visitation," and a crisis which culminated in unspeakable peace. "The day-star," he says, "arose in my heart. The spirit of mourning was taken from me. For some time I could not avoid singing Psalms wherever I was, but my joy became gradually more settled. Thus were the days of my mourning ended."

Cowper, the loftiest poet of the movement, has finely expressed this first-hand experience of God when the soul has put itself in right relations with Him:

> Admitted once to his embrace
> Thou shalt perceive that thou wast blind before.
> Thine eye shall be instructed, and thine heart,
> Made pure, shall relish with divine delight,
> Till then unfelt, what hands divine have wrought.[1]

John Haime's testimony out of his own experience is a characteristic account of the new creation which actually came to all types of people as their faith laid hold of the grace offered in the gospel of salvation. Haime had lived a rough and wicked life, sinning and feeling all the time a terror of the judgment of God for his evil ways. "Many times," he says, in his account of himself, "I have stopped in the street afraid to go on one step farther lest I should step into hell." Then came, by one of those sudden conversions, so frequent in the annals of the evangelical movement, a great experience and a new career. "One day, as I walked by the Tweed side I cried aloud, being all athirst for God, 'Oh that Thou wouldst hear my prayer, and let my cry come up before Thee!' The Lord heard. He sent a gracious answer. He lifted me out of the dungeon. He took away my sorrow and fear, and filled my soul with peace and joy in the Holy Ghost. The stream glided swiftly along, and all nature seemed to rejoice with me. I was truly free; and had I had any to guide me I need never more have come into bondage."[2]

John Nelson, a Yorkshire mason, is another good example of the transforming power and the dynamic quality of this evangelical faith. He had lived "without God," and with no expectation of getting free from his sin and sinful habits. When, however, the great act of his faith was once made, a new man was the result. "My soul seemed to breathe its life in God," he wrote of the event, "as naturally as my body breathed life in the common air." Some measure of his spirit can be taken from his calm words facing a furious mob which threatened to kill him. "You must ask my Father's permission first; for, if He has any more work for me to do, all the men in the town cannot kill me till I have done it." Being imprisoned for preaching his saving gospel, John Nelson wrote in his Journal: "My soul was as a watered garden, and I could sing praises to God all the day long; for He turned my captivity into joy and gave me to rest as well on boards, as if I had been on a bed of down. Now could I say, 'God's service is perfect freedom,' and I was carried out much in prayer that my enemies might drink of the same river of peace which my God gave so largely to me."[3]

No less remarkable is the testimony of the illiterate but extraordinary Methodist evangelist of a later period, Billy Bray. He has vividly described his entrance upon the new life of conversion as follows: "I said to the Lord: 'Thou hast said, they that ask shall receive, they that seek shall find, and to them that knock the door shall be opened, and I have faith to believe it.' In an instant the Lord made me so happy that I cannot express what I felt. I shouted for joy. I praised God with my whole heart. . . . I think this was in November 1823, but what day of the month I do not know. I remember this, that everything looked new to me, the people, the fields, the cattle, the trees. I was like a new man in a new world. I spent the greater part of my time in praising the Lord."[4] In a later passage the same evangelist describes his feelings in this quaint but expressive way: "I can't help praising the Lord. As I go along the street, I lift up one foot and it seems to say, 'Glory'; and I lift up the other, and it seems to say, 'Amen'; and so they keep up like that all the time I am walking."

Not only in the lives of leaders and evangelists who kept Journals did new power and moral strength come into play, but a new force as well found expression through this movement in the individual and social life of England. It was an intense and aggressive type of religion. It compelled men to take sides, to say yes or no, to be for or against. There was no place in it for lukewarm Laodiceans, and throughout the period of the great evangelical succession—from Wesley to Wilberforce—the movement restored religion to a first place in the thought and consideration of men. It was no longer possible, after this movement had done its work of awakening, for one to say, as Bishop Butler did in the Advertisement prefixed to his famous *Analogy*, that "it has come, I know not how, to be taken for granted by many persons that Christianity is not so much as a subject for inquiry; but that it is now at length discovered to be fictitious. And accordingly they treat it as if, in the present age, this were an agreed point

among all people of discernment; and nothing remained but
to set it up as a subject of mirth and ridicule, as it were by
reprisals, for its having so long interrupted the pleasures of
the world." Nor would a foreign visitor have said during this
movement what Montesquieu said at an earlier date: "In
England there is no religion, and the subject, if mentioned,
excites nothing but laughter." Canon Liddon is justified in
saying, as he did in his *Life of Pusey*: "The deepest and most
fervid religion in England during the first three decades of
this century [the nineteenth] was that of the evangelicals."[5]

But while this fact of new life and fresh power is undoubtedly true, and one can hardly overestimate the historical importance of the evangelical awakening, there were unmistak-
able elements of weakness in it which became more evident
when the high-tide of pristine fervour waned. Sir James
Stephen very sagely says that the movement showed "that
men might live very wisely while they reasoned very ab-
surdly,—that much practical sanctity was consistent with
much theoretical error,—that the victims of many strange
superstitions might yet have within them the living foun-
tains of eternal life, and that to a head impervious to a syl-
logism might be united a heart penetrated with the love of
God and with the love of man."[6]

The movement was never significant because of its intellectual discoveries or because it added to human thought a fresh
contribution of essential truth. It had no new stock of ideas.
It held the main body of old-fashioned orthodox views. The
dull, droning, barren clergymen, whose congregations were
sitting half asleep on Sunday and living through the week
untouched by any inspiration which came from the pulpit,
held pretty much the same set of doctrines as did these men
who woke the world from slumber and set men to living on
higher levels of moral and spiritual power. The difference was
not in creed; it was in *caloric*. In one case certain ideas which,
for the preacher, had become cold, inert and dead, were shuf-
fled back and forth as mere counters. In the other case the
ideas which were used were absolutely alive and throbbing

with quickened vitality and power. That strange experience called faith—an inner vision of reality, an assent of soul, an apprehension of things not seen—made all the difference between formality on the one hand and *élan vital* on the other. How the heightened caloric was brought into operation, why inert ideas suddenly became dynamic, will always remain, in part at least, a mystery. Mutations on any level are hard to explain. But the cardinal element here was almost certainly the contagion of kindled, fused personalities. A few persons of rare gift found a source of life and power, and they proved to be extraordinary transmitters of spiritual light and heat to others, and the age was vivified. The same ideas which in their souls glowed with the heat of intensified life had just before, and might once again, seem as ineffective as the craters of extinct volcanoes.

If, therefore, we mean by "evangelicalism" a body of doctrines, a system of theological conceptions, we shall find it difficult to maintain the position that these doctrines, and these alone, contain the eternal truth of Christianity. If we mean by it a spirit of living faith, a quickened, vivified religion, a first-hand experience of transformation and salvation by the power of Christ, we shall follow its movement with awe and reverence and we shall thank God for its prolific effects. In other words, there are in brief two main types of religion, however disguised under names and forms. There is (1) religion in its intensified, dynamic quality, and (2) there is a religion which consists of a deposit or survival of conceptions or of practice, carried along because they have become sacred habits, traditions and customs, or because they are believed to have a utilitarian value.

The line between these two types can obviously never be sharply, exactly drawn. Even the most rigid forms of the second type may have, and often do have, a fringe of live experience, and even the most vital and caloric forms of the first type carry some cooled or congealed material which is mere "survival" stuff. All branches of Christianity which become at all important and historical reveal both of these types in greater or lesser degrees. We cannot conjure with famous party names and assume off-hand that a school or system which prides itself on a sacred rubric is therefore chosen of God and elect. The real test is not to be made by canons of orthodoxy and historic theological pedigree; it is rather to be found in the dynamic quality and transforming power of one's faith. In other words, religion—religion as it concerns us in this age of the world—is a way of living, a heightening of life-force, a way of drawing upon unseen realities and of expanding the life in all its dimensions. It is a process of correspondence with man's whole *environment*, not merely with the part that occupies space; and the evidence that it is something more than superstition or invention or illusion will be found in the way it *works* as a real constructive life-force, the way it heightens life and releases energy.

There are many ways of drawing upon the invisible resources of the universe and of releasing energy to live by. Religion is one of these ways. When a person succeeds, by conscious or subconscious processes, in unifying the usually divided will, in concentrating all the inner forces upon one absorbing end, in focussing the soul's aspiration and loyalty upon one central object which meets its need and seems adequate for its nature, this surrender of self to a higher and holier Will produces the state and conditions that are essential for the flooding in of spiritual energy and for an increment and re-enforcement of one's normal powers. Everybody knows through some memorable experience what it means to lose suddenly all fear and fear-thoughts that have obsessed him and to rise up with heightened courage to face the tasks that are waiting to be done. Most persons, sometime in their lives, have seen the shadows flee away, shot through by a conquering light, and have found themselves possessed with insight and forward-looking, victorious spirit. The literature of conversion is full of records of men and women, beaten and defeated, down and out, suddenly lifted to new levels of experience, put within reach of transforming forces, flooded with transfiguring light, and becoming in the strength of this faith or this experience "twice-born" persons. This arrival of new forces of energy is, I believe, a distinguishing mark of first-hand religion, religion in its real intention.

Madame Guyon arrived at a stage of experience which she called "spiritual fecundity."[7] Unusual power of control and of endurance seemed supplied to her and, beyond that, she appeared to be able to act as a channel for currents of life and love to flow through her into others. She is no solitary example of such "fecundity." From somewhere forces not usually operating suddenly come into play and reveal their energy and their constructive activity. A person formerly "weak as any other man" becomes more than conqueror. New depths have been reached, new resources have been tapped, a fusing and kindling results, a fresh creative activity is revealed and an energizing of the whole life occurs. This energism of religion is found alike in mystical experience and in the exercise of faith as the evangelical uses the word. Wherever there is evidence of real impressive energizing, heightening of life-values, we are dealing with a vital stage of religion.

Life is a word of many meanings. It can be used in numerous aspects and in a large variety of ways. After we have exhausted the narrow biological implications of the word, we can still go on and find other significant meanings. There is an inner dimension to life which must be counted at least as real as the outer one where life-cells perform their movements. The realities which constitute for us this inner realm are our ethical and spiritual values—our loves, our loyalties, our insights, our ideals, our convictions. These are the things *by which we live*. They constitute our real personality. They make us what we are to ourselves and to those who intimately know us. Whatever permanent satisfactions we have centre round these real constituents of our inner life. To heighten and intensify these ethical and spiritual values is to increase life; to raise and expand the quality of love, of loyalty and of the soul's vision of truth is to bring a genuine increment to life itself.

When we make the test of *live* religion to be its vital, caloric, transforming, energizing quality, we mean that something comes through the religious faith and experience which ennobles love and loyalty, reinforces ideal insights and visions, something which organizes those forces in us that control, something which fortifies confidence in the mastery and final victory of truth and goodness. The individual, through his religion, becomes more joyous, more radiant, more consecrated to universal ends of goodness, more absorbed in tasks which aim to put love into full operation in the lives of men. The religious person becomes, too, at the same time, if his religion is vital, progressively grounded in his central faith that there is an eternal God at the heart of things with whom he is co-operating, an environing life which vitalizes his own and *corresponds* in mutually intimate and reciprocal ways with his own life, and promotes in the long run the triumph of the Spirit.

Evangelical religion can exhibit a notable array of testimony to the effect that "faith is the victory," that the discovery of free grace and saving love revealed in Christ is energizing and brings spiritual fecundity. Luther's famous account of faith is borne out in the experience of multitudes of persons: "Faith is a living, deliberate confidence in the grace of God, so certain that for it one could die a thousand deaths. And such confidence makes the believer joyous, intrepid and full of cheer towards God and all creation."[8]

The way in which *meaning* suddenly flashes into an awakened consciousness and brings new insight and power is, again, finely told in Luther's *Table-Talk:* "When a fellow-monk one day repeated the words of the Creed, 'I believe in the forgiveness of sins,' *I saw the Scripture in an entirely new light; and straightway I felt as if I were born anew. It was as if I had found the door of Paradise thrown wide open!*" The world is very familiar now, in these anniversary years of the great events of Luther's heroic period, with the epoch-making discovery which turned Luther from a contemplative monk into a world-shaking Reformer. Formerly it was supposed that the

transforming discovery was made on the "holy stairway" in
Rome. It is now generally conceded by historians that the new
insight came to the monk while he was preparing his lectures
on the Epistle to the Romans, probably about 1515. He had
long been struggling over the meaning of "justification" and
he had puzzled in vain over the way in which a "merciless and
angry" God could be appeased and satisfied. Suddenly the
meaning of the apostolic words, "the just shall live by faith,"
surged into his mind. He realized in a flash of inner light that
God meets man's needs with grace and not with wrath, in a
word that God is like Christ and so forgives. It seemed to
him in the joy of this illumination as though the gates of
paradise had opened wide.

But we are in quite another world when we pass over from
this first-hand experience of energized awakening to the cooled
lava stage of inherited, transmitted doctrine. Evangelical
Christianity very easily drops to this lower secondary stage,
and those who are antagonistic to it for the most part know it
only as a dry formulated system of theology, arbitrarily set
up as the only way of salvation. It is obvious that no type of
religion can ever hold its place in the continuous life of men
and generations which does not stand for positive, distinctive
truth and carry along well-defined ideas, so that in one sense
there can be no religion without *doctrine*, that is without a
formulation of truth. Nobody wants a religion which is mere
enthusiasm, awakened emotion, undirected fire of the spirit!
These emotional bursts end invariably in dissipated energy
and disillusionment. Intellectual content and control of the
will toward adequate ends of life are absolutely essential for
the formation of a religion of power.

The difficulty with evangelicalism in this respect has been
that its expounders and defenders have assumed, or at least
have seemed to assume, that certain doctrines have a magical
efficacy for salvation, as formerly contact with holy relics was
supposed to have, or as the mediation of the ordained priest
of the Middle Ages was believed to have, and these sacred
doctrines have tended to become to their minds a good in

themselves and an end in themselves. To hold those particular views, to assent to those essential doctrines, to say "yes"
to that exalted scheme of salvation, is supposed to advance
the soul in some mysterious way toward its eternal peace.
Without meaning to be antinomian and with no intention of
encouraging slackness in moral life, the advocates of this
system do, nevertheless, unwittingly foster the impression
that acceptance of doctrine brings salvation, and the natural
effect has been and is that the essential business of moral
conquest and spiritual transformation slips away from the
centre into the fringe. Preaching tends to become, at least
on the part of the smaller and less prophetic preachers, a
repetitious expounding of doctrine, a wearisome re-statement
of views, and by a well-known psychological principle the
minds of the listeners become "ichored" over and callous to
the words. What has once been charged with the vital quality
of awakened faith, surprise, discovery, truth, is now familiar,
reiterated preacher's phrases, somewhat sleepily assented to as
a view which must be in some way believed. Thus by the
cooling processes of habit and custom and repetition the
original power tends to wane and vanish.

The fundamental assumption of this type of religion that
there are no new discoveries to be made, that nothing new is
to be expected, that the returns of essential truth are all in,
works in the direction of lethargy and stagnation. It is in
this respect like the situation to which the schoolmen were
doomed. They could not expect to discover anything by their
philosophical search; they could only hope to find fresh ways
of verifying *the truth* once for all revealed. The present-day
student is apt to leave these schoolmen on their long mediaeval
loop, and he leaps over from the dynamic ancients to the no
less dynamic moderns. The very basic assumption that the
way of human salvation can be put into a fixed and unchanging formulation and can be passed on from everlasting to everlasting in static form dooms it to become, on the part of those
who accept it, a thing taken for granted on a basis of authority and assented to without much release of inner energy.

A graver difficulty appears, however, with a system like this. It is compelled in our time to face the insistent question of *fact*. Is this body of doctrine, claimed to be essential, able to resist all attempts to doubt it? Does it stand the severest "chemic tests"? Has it come triumphantly through the crucible of critical examination? Is one bound, if he would be a sincere disciple of Christ and if he hopes for full redemption from sin, to believe just this one set of doctrines as truth and nothing but truth? An unconditional affirmative cannot be given to these questions. The account of human nature upon which the eighteenth-century evangelicals insisted has been seriously shaken by the gradual progress of verified knowledge. The traditional origin of the race from a lofty, exalted progenitor who fell by a single act of disobedience and involved the whole race in ruin and in moral depravity can be held only by persons who decline to accept the conclusions reached by the entire body of scientific scholars. The whole conception of man and of man's inner history on the planet has undergone a profound change to which a religion that is to survive and to speak to the condition of the growing world must adjust itself. This advancement of knowledge, this progress of science, has, it should be added, disproved no essential religious truth. It has not sapped or mined at any point the fundamental basis of spiritual life or saving faith, but it has unmistakably made clear that this particular theological account is built on tradition and not on historical fact. The narrative out of which the theory has been constructed is lofty epic literature, full of creative suggestion and laden with spiritual truth, but not factual, literal history, containing an infallible genetic account of the race. These primitive narratives do give a profoundly significant view of the collision between instinct and moral insight and they furnish an impressive revelation of the truth that one cannot pass from pure innocence to a life of moral issues without meeting temptation, without facing the possibility of sin, without experience of inner struggle. In this immemorial collision conscience is born, knowledge of good and evil is formed. This moral crisis, whether in the case of the individual or of the race, is both a fall and a rise. Once having chosen by an act of will a course of life, once having left the happy unconscious state of instinctive inno-cence behind, one can never go back to it. For better or for worse the race to which we belong, the man we know, has come to a stage of life on a level of moral choices. We no longer blindly obey the push of unreflective instinct. We have entered upon a career of struggle and suffering, of defeats as well as of victories, of aspiration and ideals in conflict with lower impulses. Our world is henceforth a checker-board world of black and white.

But just as surely this stage of moral collision is a rise, is an advance. There is no other way to "make man." It is through the purgatorial process of life like ours that the mean-ing and distinction of sin and holiness stand clearly forth. In order to be *good* a man must learn to prefer a higher course when an alternative lower one confronts him. He cannot be pushed into goodness. He must love goodness and feel its attraction and choose it. This great chance at the highest kind of life has come to us, with all its moral dignity—but it carries with it, too, the momentous possibilities of failure, defeat and loss. We are, in short, in a world where sin is an appalling fact, a world which no rose-water remedy will cure; and the evangelical is right in emphasizing the awfulness of sin and the disease of will that inheres in it, but he neglects to take account of the mighty spiritual forces which are planted in the very structure of man's soul, and he ignores the diviner aspects of life which are rooted and grounded in the moral nature of struggling, suffering humanity.

A grave misinterpretation somewhat similar to this misin-terpretation of human nature runs through the whole system. It is constructed to fit a dualistic universe, a two-world scheme. Its treatment of Christ, its theory of Scripture, its conception of salvation, are all worked out to correspond with that unsatisfactory and inadequate two-compartment view of the world, and it fails to tally with the expanded and transformed world-view which has become the intellectual inheritance of this age. The central truths of religion, if they are to guide the will and form the character, control the impulses and be an inspiration to the ideals of men to-day, must be interpreted and formulated in harmony with all that we know to be true about man and about the world in which his life is bound up. It is the prophetic task of the religious leaders of our time to work out this adjustment, and to re-express in vital, convincing form the eternal truth about God and the soul, about Christ and man's salvation.

All that is true and great at the heart of the evangelical movement, and there is much that is true and great, must be conserved. The overwhelming sense of God, the staggering consciousness of sin, the transforming discovery of divine grace, the joyous assurance of forgiveness which characterize the great evangelicals are essential features of any profound spiritual experience. The insistence which one finds in the evangelical movement that religion be given a first place in life, that Christ shall have the supremacy, must be maintained. The exalted conviction which belongs to the evangelical faith that religion has to do with a world of transcendent reality and affects eternal destiny must not be allowed to drop away. No religion which is merely subjective, a one-sided affair and unattached to any super-temporal reality, will ever build the spiritual world we ask for. But all these central features of a live religion can be conserved in a spiritual movement that is essentially mystical much better than in a system which is essentially static and forensic as the one under consideration tends to become. If we are determined to find sources of vital growth and expanding power we must keep close to the actual elemental nature of the soul itself. If we are to have theology we must have a theology which conforms through and through with sound psychology and which squares at every point with verified truth in all departments.

There can, I think, be little question that the mystical basis of religion fits better than any other with what we know of the verified facts of life. I mean by "mystical basis" that feature of religion which attaches to the soul's direct testimony of relation with God. Our senses, in the last resort, *i.e.* in ultimate analysis, deal only with molecular motion. We do not, and cannot, "perceive" in the outward world any reality to which we could properly apply the word God. Nor will any "process" of inner consciousness by itself ever give the experience of an absolute and eternal reality to which we could ascribe the ineffable Name. But notwithstanding that necessary concession, there is something inherently bound up with all self-conscious experience which has inevitable reference to a transcendent super-temporal reality. We cannot live and think without passing beyond the finite objects of sense and the ephemeral processes of consciousness and without fusing ourselves in with a larger inclusive whole of reality which abides and endures. If we were sundered from this larger whole, if we lost our connection and correspondence, we should lose ourselves and all we know. We cannot *live* a moment without being more than ourselves. We cannot go forward toward the life we want without projecting the tentacles of the soul on into some firm reality beyond and yet within our experience. We make all our advances by trusting the soul's "invincible surmise." We keep seeking God because we are all the time finding Him.

Then there are those rarer fusing, vitalizing experiences which come oftener to some than to others, when the larger whole of reality with which we are always in contact seems to become resurgent and to flood back into our inner channels and to charge us with unwonted vital energy. Even more important, perhaps, is the evidence of God which comes in quiet ways to the soul through the moral and spiritual tasks of a lifetime, and through the slow formation of a higher nature within that triumphs over lower impulses and instincts. We become, without quite knowing how, the finite organs of a Spirit like ourselves, and yet unspeakably vaster, who is the environment of all awakened spirits and the Life of all spiritual lives. We may not be able to *prove* to others that we have found God in these experiences, but while we feel the floods of life and the tides of love we do not care much for proofs.

It is here, on this testimony of the soul, that the religion of the mystical type is founded. What is wrong with man it finds revealed within, and what is divinely possible for man it finds, too, implied in the intimations of the soul. And with this sure clue it turns to history, which is the record of that continuous humanity of which we are each fragmentary units. In this wider life of man the revelation of sin and of divine grace which is in part unveiled within us becomes more luminous. Prophets give us personal testimonies which far out-top our own, but which at the same time confirm our own discovery. One historical Figure stands out in solitary splendour. In Jesus Christ we have the supreme confirmation of our most significant inner intimations and discoveries. The conviction of connection with God reached in Him its highest certainty. He felt Himself to be the instrument and organ of divine manifestation in unparalleled degree. Grace, forgiving, suffering, love, which was incarnate in Him, rose upon His consciousness as the central fact in the nature and character of God, and He made it in His representative life and death so vivid and dynamic that it is burned forever into the spiritual consciousness of those who love Him and follow Him.

All the theological terms which characterize religious movements in history are more or less partial and one-sided. They merely give emphasis—often excessive emphasis—to one aspect of truth and overlook or neglect other aspects quite as important as the one that is singled out and starred. Moreover these terms are too apt to become party watchwords and battle-cries within the Church. "Evangelical" or "mystical" is an unnecessary alternative. A complete religion, a full-rounded Christianity will be both evangelical and mystical, provided, of course, that the term evangelical is used in its deeper and truer sense. Narrow, partial, exclusive forms and formulations must pass away and give place to types of religion which express in ever-growing degree the whole meaning of life and the whole range of truth. The richer and more inclusive types, just because they are rich and inclusive, bear clear testimony to the spiritual potentiality of man, to the essential junction of the human and the divine, to the prophetic and oracular gifts of the soul, and at the same time they recognize and proclaim the unique revelation of God in Scripture, and the supreme unveiling of His nature and character in that one perfect personal Life which was both divine and human.

The pages which follow this Introduction will not be mainly concerned with theological views. They will aim rather to present the complex life, the social ideals, the currents and movements of a religious body in England and America, working out its spiritual hopes and shaping its destiny during the last two centuries. The only reason for concentrating here upon somewhat abstract aspects of thought, when more interesting matters were at hand, is that historically these abstract aspects have by the actors themselves been raised to a place of central importance, and have been dominating factors in the unfolding movement of Quaker history. Life itself is concrete, and religion, in so far as it is a vital affair, is a concrete way of life with unique and original features in each individual life. It cannot be reduced to its general and abstract forms without a loss of the essential features that make it a thing of interest and wonder. But these concrete and personal lives of ours, with all their dramatic and unique possibilities, are immensely influenced and shaped by the abstract principles, the theories of truth and the systems of thought, which we adopt as a working basis of life and action. Here is the key to much of the tragedy and to some of the comedy of life. Systems of thought are like cathedrals, very slowly built up, and when once they are wrought into shape they have an abiding and persisting character. They do not yield at once in the presence of new discoveries, they do not alter easily to fit the complex facts of inner experience and of growing, expanding truth. They *hold* even when they have become inadequate to express the richer concrete life of a new time. For that reason one cannot write the history of a people as it really was without serious consideration of what has been called "the universe of thought" under which the people were living when they made their history. Life is not a series of dots, a shower of shot, nor is it a sporadic, capricious, un-ordered manifold of incidents. It is an integral and unified affair, controlled and directed by ideas and purposes which bind it together, and organize it into a significant whole. The binding principles and unifying purposes are therefore momentous matters which cannot be neglected for the sake of cataloguing the bright and interesting purple patches which attract attention and make the more abstract features seem dull and dreary.

NOTES

1. William Cowper, *The Task*, Bk. V.
2. Fitchetts, *Wesley and his Century* (New York, 1912), p. 235.
3. John Nelson's *Journal*, p. 172.
4. W. F. Bourne, *The King's Son: a Memoir of Billy Bray* (London: Hamilton, Adams & Co., 1887), p. 9.
5. *Life of Pusey*, vol. i. p. 255.
6. Stephen's *Essays in Ecclesiastical Biography* (London, 1868), p. 441.
7. *Later Periods of Quakerism*, p. 87, note.
8. Preface to the *Epistle to the Romans*.

BOOKS BY AND ABOUT RUFUS M. JONES

Available 1963

A Call to What is Vital
New York, Macmillan, 1948.   143 p.

The Faith and Practice of the Quakers
London, Methuen, 1927.   181 p.
Philadelphia, Philadelphia Yearly Meeting, 1958.   Paperback

The Later Periods of Quakerism
London, Macmillan, 1921.   2 vols., 1020 p.

The Life and Message of George Fox, 1624–1924, A Tercentenary Address
New York, Macmillan, 1924.   31 p.

The Quakers in the American Colonies
London, Macmillan, 1911.   603 p.
New York, Russell and Russell, 1962.

The Shepherd Who Missed the Manger
Garden City, N. Y., Doubleday, Doran, 1941.   28 p. Pamphlet
Philadelphia, Friends Book Store, 1948.

Spirit in Man
Stanford University, Calif., Stanford University Press, 1941.   70 p.
Berkeley, Calif., Peacock Press, 1962.   79 p.

Spiritual Energies in Daily Life
New York, Macmillan, 1922.   179 p.   1936.   Revised edition, 196 p.
Philadelphia, Philadelphia Yearly Meeting, 1961.   Paperback

Spiritual Reformers in the 16th and 17th Centuries
London, Macmillan, 1914.   362 p.
Boston, Beacon Press, 1959.   Paperback

The Story of George Fox
New York, Macmillan, 1919.   169 pp.
Philadelphia, Friends Book Store, 1943.

ANTHOLOGY

Rufus Jones Speaks to Our Time, An Anthology, Edited by Harry Emerson Fosdick
New York, Macmillan, 1951.   289 p.   1961.   Paperback
London, Bannisdale Press, 1933.   286 p.

Thou Dost Open Up My Life, Selections from the Rufus Jones Collection, Edited by Mary Hoxie Jones
Wallingford, Pa., Pendle Hill Pamphlet number 127, 1963.   40 p.

BIOGRAPHY

Friend of Life, The Biography of Rufus M. Jones, by Elizabeth Gray Vining
Philadelphia, Lippincott, 1958. 347 p.
London, Michael Joseph, 1959. 350 p.

Rufus M. Jones, A Biographical Sketch, by Mary Hoxie Jones
London, Friends Home Service Committee, 1955. 70 p. Pamphlet

All books may be ordered from

FRIENDS BOOK STORE
302 Arch Street, Philadelphia 6, Pa.